I0529090

THE TRUTH SERIES

TRUTH ABOUT THE TRINITY

Exploring Christian Doctrines with Love and Logic

David E. Longenecker

Truth About the Trinity
Exploring Christian Doctrines with Love and Logic

Published by DELministries, Inc.
P.O. Box 465, Sadsburyville, PA 19369

Library of Congress Control Number: 2025904013
ISBN: 979-8-9927649-0-1

Unless otherwise noted, Scripture quotations are from the *New Heart English Bible (NHEB)*, public domain.

Scripture quotations marked KJV are from *The Holy Bible, King James Version*, public domain.

Scripture quotations marked ESV are from *The Holy Bible, English Standard Version® (ESV)*, copyright © 2001 by Crossway. Used by permission. All rights reserved.

Divine pronouns are capitalized, and brackets or bold text have been added by the author for clarity and reflection. This book reflects the author's perspective and is not a substitute for pastoral guidance or personal study of Scripture.

For more about *The Truth Series*, visit:
www.JesusConquers.com

Printed in the United States of America.

Table of Contents

Introduction: The Truth That Changes Everything

Seeing God Clearly Transforms Your Life

Have you ever believed in God, yet felt He was distant—like there must be more to knowing Him than what you've experienced?

Maybe you've sensed His presence, but something still feels missing.

What if the real barrier isn't your faith—but your view of God?

You pray, but wonder if He hears.

You trust Him—yet He still feels far away.

Could it be that your view of God is clouded, keeping you from *fully* experiencing His love, joy, and peace?

Picture standing at the edge of an endless ocean. Waves stretch beyond the horizon—powerful, overwhelming. You wade in, feel the spray, touch the water. But no matter how deep you go, its vastness remains.

Encountering God is like that.

He is infinite in majesty, yet near in love.

Not just a concept to study, but a Person to know.

The Trinity isn't something you decode—it's Someone you encounter.

Nothing shapes your life more than how you see and experience God.

If you see Him as distant, you'll feel abandoned in trials.

If you reduce Him to human terms, worship loses its wonder.

If you misunderstand Him, your faith may falter when life doesn't go as expected.

But what if you could see God clearly—without the barriers that cloud your relationship with Him?

Many imagine God as far off or unknowable.

But the Bible reveals something radically different:

God wants to be known!

From the beginning, He has revealed Himself—not as a vague force or abstract idea, but as a living, relational God.

And He has made Himself known most fully through the Trinity: His unfolding self-revelation as Father, Son, and Spirit —a truth that has shaped the Christian faith for centuries.

So how do we see God as He truly is?

This book is your invitation to that journey.

The Mystery of God's Oneness Revealed

The Bible declares with striking clarity that God is one:

Hear, Israel: the LORD is our God, the LORD is one.
— Deuteronomy 6:4

Yet from the beginning, that oneness unfolds in mystery.

In Genesis, God speaks creation into existence through His Word, while His Spirit hovers over the waters, breathing life and sustaining all things:

> *In the beginning God created the heavens and the earth...*
> *God's Spirit was hovering over the surface of the waters.*
> *And God said, "Let there be light."*
>
> — *Genesis 1:1—3*

This pattern—the Father speaking, the Word going forth, the Spirit moving—appears again and again.

This mystery comes into full view at Jesus' baptism:

> *And Jesus, when He was baptized... the heavens were*
> *opened to Him, and He saw the Spirit of God descending as*
> *a dove, and... a voice out of the heavens said, "This is My*
> *beloved Son."*
>
> — *Matthew 3:16—17*

Here, we don't just read about the Trinity—we see it.

For centuries, Christians have wrestled with how these truths fit together. Scripture teaches that God is one, yet reveals Him as Father, Son, and Spirit.

So...who is God, really?

Not theologically—but personally.

Intimately. Eternally.

Why the Trinity Feels Like a Puzzle

Why does the Trinity feel more like a puzzle to solve than a Person to love?

For many, the confusion doesn't come from Scripture—but from how theology evolved over time. (*See Appendix A for a fuller timeline of the key councils and what they defended*).

Early Christians experienced the Trinity firsthand: praying to the Father, following the Son, walking in the Spirit's power.

Their faith wasn't rooted in abstract theories, but in real encounters with God.

Over time, well-meaning theologians turned to Greek philosophy—especially its view of "perfection" as impersonal, unmoving, and detached—to explain God's nature.

But this made God feel more like a formula than a Father who knows us by name.

What if the Trinity is simpler—and more relational—than we've imagined?

Some of the earliest Christian teachers—like Theophilus and Tertullian—believed so.

They described the Trinity in deeply relational terms and warned the Church not to mix God's nature with Greek philosophy. (*See Appendix B for their insights and warnings*).

The Trinity is not a riddle to be solved—it's the deepest revelation of God's love.

The Father calls you into His eternal love.

The Son embodies that love, uniting divine glory with human weakness.

The Spirit fills you with that same love, making God's presence real and personal.

When we see God this way, theology stops being a subject to study and becomes an invitation to relationship.

A Clearer Vision of God Changes Your Life

Seeing God clearly doesn't just shape your beliefs—it transforms your experience of Him.

It deepens your faith.

It reshapes your prayers.

It brings intimacy with God that anchors your heart in every storm.

Misunderstand Him, and even the strongest faith will begin to waver.

See the Father as distant, and you'll feel unworthy of His love.

See Jesus as just a teacher, and you'll miss the power of His sacrifice.

Overlook the Spirit, and you'll live as though God is far away—rather than dwelling within you.

But when you see God as He truly is—one God revealing Himself as Father, Son, and Spirit, moving in perfect love—your faith becomes unshakable.

Your prayers grow bold.

Your worship comes alive.

Your daily walk is filled with His presence.

How to Encounter God in a Deeper Way

This book isn't just about learning—it's about transformation.

It's an invitation to move beyond theology into real encounter.

To not just believe in God—but to *know* Him.

To see the Father's love clearly.

To walk in the Son's redemption fully.

To live by the Spirit's power boldly.

This is the journey before you.

In these pages, you'll encounter familiar language—Father, Son, and Spirit—because Scripture uses these terms.

But unlike later theology shaped by Greek categories, this book roots them in the unfolding story of God's self-revelation.

If a word feels familiar, keep reading.

You may come to see it in a whole new light—not through the lens of philosophy, but through the living rhythm of Scripture itself.

Step by step, this book will guide the way:

- **Part One** lays the foundation—exploring God's oneness and the mystery of the Trinity.

- **Part Two** uncovers how the Father, Son, and Spirit actively move in creation, redemption, and your daily life.

- **Part Three** reveals how a clearer vision of God transforms your prayer, worship, and experience of His love.

He knows your name.

He sees your struggles.

And He is calling you deeper.

The ocean stretches before you. Will you step in?

PART 1—ENCOUNTERING GOD

The Trinity's True Foundation

Chapter 1: Recovering the Trinity of the Bible

Why the Trinity Is Hard to Understand

Have you ever tried to explain the Trinity—only to find that the more you spoke, the more confused you became?

For centuries, believers have wrestled with this mystery, often seeing God as a puzzle rather than a Person.

> **The Trinity isn't just a doctrine—it's the foundation of a living relationship with God.**

The Bible doesn't present the Trinity as a complex equation to decode, but as the heartbeat of divine love—a God who is Father, Son, and Spirit, eternally giving, revealing, and inviting us into fellowship with Himself.

So why does it feel so complicated?

Terms like *coeternal, coequal,* and *eternal generation* were meant to clarify the Trinity—but for many, they only raise more questions.

Where did these ideas come from?

And why do they seem to complicate what Scripture presents so simply?

In this chapter, we'll explore how the Church's understanding of the Trinity developed—and how Greek philosophy influenced that process.

More importantly, we'll return to Scripture, *where the fog begins to lift*, and rediscover a clearer, more beautiful vision of God as Father, Son, and Spirit.

Did Philosophy Complicate the Trinity?

As Christianity spread through the Roman Empire, believers encountered a world steeped in abstract reasoning and philosophical ideas about divinity.

In their effort to safeguard the Gospel from heresy, Early Church leaders began to draw heavily from Greek philosophy.

Augustine, writing near the end of the fourth century, captured this approach when he said:

> *If those who are called philosophers, and especially the Platonists, have said anything that is true and in harmony with our faith, we are not only not to shrink from it, but to **claim it for our own use**.*

— Augustine, *On Christian Doctrine*, Book 2, Chapter 40

Though well-intentioned, this strategy introduced categories foreign to Scripture—turning the Trinity from a relational reality into a metaphysical puzzle.

But what if God was never meant to be this complicated?

What if true clarity doesn't come from Greek philosophy—but from the story Scripture tells?

When we let Scripture shape our understanding, the Trinity stops being an intellectual puzzle and becomes a living, dynamic reality—a God who desires to be known.

*This is everlasting life, **that they may know You**, the only true God, and Him whom You sent, Jesus Christ.*

— John 17:3

How Greek Thought Shaped Theology

Greek philosophy profoundly influenced how early theologians framed God's nature.

Plato—perhaps the most influential of them all—viewed eternity as timeless and changeless, and perfection as existing beyond relationship.

His ultimate reality, the "Forms" or "the Good," was abstract and impersonal—more of an idea than a living, relational God.

But this contradicts Scripture!

The Bible reveals God as both eternal and deeply personal:

He answers prayers (2 Chronicles 7:14).
Responds to repentance (Jonah 3:10).
And even grieves (Genesis 6:6).

God's perfection is not cold detachment—it's expressed through love.

Likewise, eternity isn't frozen in a static "eternal now." It pulses with joy, divine action, and unfolding purpose.

In Revelation 5–6, the Lamb receives a scroll, and as each seal is opened, God's redemptive plan unfolds—both in time and eternity. Though time unfolds differently, eternity is anything but static or changeless.

While Plato envisioned divine perfection as stillness, Scripture reveals it through movement, relationship, and love.

Recognizing the deep divide between philosophy and Scripture, the Apostle Paul, Theophilus, and Tertullian each sounded the alarm—warning the Church not to mix philosophical speculation with the truth of Scripture. (*See Appendix B*).

The Trinity: A Historic Struggle

As Greek ideas seeped into Christian thought, the Church found itself struggling to express divine truth in foreign terms.

By the fourth century, questions about Jesus' identity had reached a boiling point—forcing the Church to respond.

Was Jesus Really God? The Ancient Debate

Around this time, Arius—a pastor from Alexandria—argued that the Son was not eternal, but created.

He pointed to verses like:

> *For God so loved the world, that He gave His only **begotten** Son.*
> *— John 3:16, KJV*

> *Who is the image of the invisible God, the **Firstborn** over all creation.*
> *— Colossians 1:15*

Arius concluded: *There was a time when the Son was not.*

Influenced by Greek philosophy—especially the belief that anything with a beginning couldn't be divine—he reasoned that Jesus couldn't be *fully* God, leading him into heresy.

How the Council of Nicaea Confirmed Christ's Divinity

In 325 AD, Church leaders gathered at the Council of Nicaea to resolve the controversy.

They affirmed that the Son is *of the same substance* as the Father—fully divine, not a lesser being.

To defend this truth against Arianism, they introduced philosophical terms such as:

Coeternal – The Son has no beginning or end.
Coequal – The Son is fully equal with the Father.

Though these terms defended Christ's divinity in a Greek-speaking world, they often overshadowed Scripture's simpler, more relational vision of God.

How Greek Philosophy Distorted the Trinity

Though the Council preserved Christ's divinity, Greek concepts continued to shape how the Trinity was explained.

Coeternal echoed Plato's belief that divinity must exist in a timeless state—but Scripture reveals eternity as alive with action and unfolding purpose.

Coequal reflected Plato's assumption that perfection requires sameness—but Scripture reveals a unity that flourishes through distinction: the Father and the Son are one, yet not identical (John 5:19).

To further defend Christ's divinity, later theologians introduced the idea of *eternal generation*—that the Son is eternally begotten of the Father, coming forth without beginning or end.

(We'll explore the meaning of "begotten" more fully in Chapter 4—not as a complex theological concept, but as a pic-

ture of Christ's unique role in redemptive history).

Eternal generation was meant to describe the unique relationship between the Father and Son, while avoiding any sense of time or inferiority. Yet this language left many confused:

- If the Father "eternally begets" the Son, does that suggest the Son had a starting point?
- Does this language unintentionally imply that the Son is lesser than the Father?
- How well does this align with Scripture's relational picture?

In the end, this philosophical language made God harder to grasp—rather than easier to know. (*For a deeper look at how the early councils fought to protect key truths—and the lasting tensions they left behind—see Appendix A*).

The Trinity: A Relationship, Not a Theory

The Bible doesn't define Jesus' divinity in abstract terms. It reveals Him through relationship.

> *He* [the Son] *is the radiance of His* [the Father's] *glory, the very image of His substance.*
>
> — *Hebrews 1:3*

Unlike angels, humans, or anything created, Jesus alone comes forth from the Father as His ultimate self-revelation (John 1:14). This sets Him apart from everything in Heaven and on earth.

24

He doesn't just teach us about God—He brings us face to face with Him.

Through the Son:

The unapproachable God draws near.
The invisible God becomes visible.
The unknowable God makes Himself known.

To know Jesus is to *encounter* the living God.

How the Father Reveals Jesus as God

The Father affirms Jesus' divinity through three undeniable truths:

1. The Father commands the angels to worship the Son.

When God brings His Firstborn into the world, He says, "Let all God's angels worship Him."

— Hebrews 1:6

Worship belongs to God alone—yet the Father commands all of Heaven to worship the Son. This is a clear and unmistakable declaration: Jesus is fully divine.

2. The Son rules over all creation.

All authority has been given to Me in Heaven and on earth.

— Matthew 28:18

Jesus holds divine authority over everything in existence—a power that belongs only to God Himself.

3. The Son is the supreme judge.

The Father judges no one, but He has given all judgment to the Son.

— *John 5:22*

Only God can judge the world. Yet the Father has entrusted this role to the Son—further affirming that Jesus is God.

Because of this, the Father declares:

All men should honor the Son, even as they honor the Father.

— *John 5:23*

Arius, influenced by Greek ideas, missed what Scripture declares plainly:

To see the Son is to see the Father.
To know the Son is to know the living God.

The answers to Arius's doubts were in Scripture all along.

How the Trinity Transforms Your Faith

God is not distant or abstract. He is personal, present, and deeply engaged in your life.

When we let Scripture—not philosophy—shape our understanding, we begin to see God as He truly is:

Dynamic, not static.
Loving, not detached.
Relational, not impersonal.

26

This is the heartbeat of the Trinity:

The Father draws near through the Son.
The Son reveals the Father and redeems humanity.
The Spirit makes the Father's love and the Son's presence real in our lives.

> **The Trinity is not a theory to decode—but an invitation into the very life of God.**

Seeing God clearly doesn't just inform your faith—it transforms it.
The Father calls you into His love.
The Son makes the invisible God visible.
The Spirit draws you closer every day.

> **You were made for this relationship.**

To know the Son is to know the Father.
To walk in the Spirit is to walk in the Father's presence.
And in that clarity, you'll realize—He's been closer than you ever imagined.

Looking Ahead

We've cleared away the source of the confusion—recovering a vision of the Trinity that is relational, biblical, and alive.

But before we explore how God is revealed as Father, Son, and Spirit, we must return to the foundation that shaped all true worship.

In the next chapter, we'll stand with Israel at the base of Sinai—where God thundered His identity into history:

The LORD is one.

This is the heartbeat of devotion.

Only when we see God's oneness clearly can we begin to behold His fullness—revealed in the Son and the Spirit.

This understanding will transform how you see and trust God in every moment of your life.

Reflection and Study Guide

Chapter 1: Recovering the Trinity of the Bible

*This is everlasting life, that they may know You,
the only true God. — John 17:3*

Questions for Reflection

- **Cultural Influence:** How have tradition and cultural assumptions shaped your view of the Trinity? In what ways does Scripture confirm—or challenge—those ideas?

- **The Role of Philosophy:** Greek philosophy shaped theological terms like *eternal generation* and *coeternal*. Do you think philosophy has helped—or hindered—our understanding of God?

- **God's Relational Nature:** Instead of seeing the Trinity as a puzzle, how does viewing God as relational and dynamic impact your faith?

Key Takeaways

- **The Trinity is Biblical:** It is revealed in God's Word —not created by Greek philosophy.

- **God is Relational:** Father, Son, and Spirit are one God, united in perfect love and action.

- **Seeing Clearly:** Removing philosophical filters allows us to encounter the living God—not just a theological idea.

Practical Application

- **Pray in Alignment with Scripture:** Let Jesus' pattern shape your prayers:

  1. **Pray to the Father**—the source of life and love.
  2. **Pray through the Son**—who reveals the Father.
  3. **Pray by the Spirit**—for guidance, power, and transformation (Ephesians 6:18, John 14:13–14).

- **Study with Fresh Eyes:** Choose one passage (John 1:1, John 14:26, 1 Corinthians 8:6) and reflect on how the Father, Son, and Spirit work as one.

- **Challenge Assumptions:** Take time to journal your current understanding of the Trinity. Which parts may have been shaped more by tradition or culture than by Scripture itself? What might God be inviting you to see more clearly?

Chapter 2: Worshiping the One True God

Why God's Oneness Matters

You stand at the foot of Mount Sinai.

The ground trembles.

Thunder crashes.

Fire engulfs the mountain.

Smoke thickens the air.

Then, through the storm, a voice—powerful and unrelenting—declares:

> *I am the LORD your God, who brought you out of the land of Egypt, out of the house of bondage.*
>
> *— Exodus 20:2*

This moment wasn't just about awe or power.

It was a defining revelation.

God wasn't revealing Himself as one god among many.

He was declaring Himself as the *only* true God—supreme over all creation.

From that day forward, Israel carried a truth that set them apart from every nation on earth:

> *The LORD is our God, the LORD is one.*
>
> *— Deuteronomy 6:4*

This declaration—known as the *Shema*—became the foundation of biblical faith. But in Hebrew, Shema means more than "hear."

It means:

Listen. Pay attention. Respond.

It calls for wholehearted devotion—alignment of heart, soul, and strength with God's will.

In a world flooded with idols, the Shema became Israel's battle cry.

To say *"Yahweh* alone is God" wasn't abstract theology—it was defiance.

A bold rejection of every false god and rival claim on their worship.

But the Shema wasn't just about belief—it was about love:

> *Love the LORD your God with all your heart, and with all your soul, and with all your might.*
>
> *— Deuteronomy 6:5*

Before we can begin to grasp the mystery of the Trinity, we must first stand in awe of this unshakable truth:

> *I am the LORD, and there is no other. Besides Me, there is no God.*
>
> *— Isaiah 45:5*

This is where worship begins—not with theological debate, but with *surrender.*

In His presence, self-sufficiency fades, idols crumble, and worship rises from the ashes.

The Shema: A Revolutionary Declaration

The ancient world was filled with gods.

Every nation had its idols.

Every city had its shrines.

And every people pledged loyalty to their own deities.

In that world, the Shema was more than a statement—it was a revolution:

Yahweh alone is the true and living God—sovereign over all creation.

This truth struck at the heart of ancient religion.

It set Israel apart as the people of the one true God—unrivaled, unchanging, and without equal.

Through the prophet Isaiah, God thundered again:

I am the First, and I am the Last; and besides Me, there is no God.

— Isaiah 44:6

For Israel, worshiping Yahweh wasn't just religion.

It was loyalty.

To say "The LORD is one" was to draw a line in the sand—a refusal to give heart, trust, or worship to anyone else.

It was a radical act of faith.

And that same battle continues today.

Our idols no longer look like golden calves or carved statues.

Today, they disguise themselves as power, success, image, wealth, relationships, and self-reliance.

Anything that takes God's rightful place in our hearts becomes an idol.

The Shema still calls us to the same unwavering devotion.

It still calls for a single-hearted worship of the one true God.

> *Do not have other gods before Me.*
> *— Exodus 20:3*

The question remains:

Does your worship belong *fully* to Him?

How Jesus Reveals the One True God

The New Testament doesn't replace the truth of God's oneness—it unfolds its depth and fulfillment in Christ.

The Shema remains the foundation of our faith.

But now we see the Father, Son, and Spirit acting in perfect unity.

Picture sunlight pouring through a window:

The sun is the source—the origin of light and life.

The light reveals—making the sun visible.

Its warmth carries the sun's presence—bringing life and renewal.

In the same way:

The Father is the source—unseen, eternal, Creator of all.

The Son makes Him known—revealing the Father in human form.

The Spirit carries His presence—bringing His life and transformation into our hearts.

When asked about the greatest commandment, Jesus reaffirmed the Shema:

> *"Which commandment is the greatest of all?" Jesus answered, "The first is, 'Hear, Israel, the Lord our God, the Lord is one.'"*
> *— Mark 12:28–29*

And Paul, under the inspiration of the Spirit, revealed its stunning fulfillment:

> *There is one God, the Father, from whom are all things, and we for Him; and one Lord, Jesus Christ, through whom are all things, and we live through Him.*
> *— 1 Corinthians 8:6*

Paul doesn't present two gods.

He reveals that the one true God is made known through Father and Son.

The Father is Yahweh—Creator, sustainer, the One worthy of worship (John 4:23). The Son is His image—the visible expression of the invisible God (Hebrews 1:3). Jesus is not a second God. He is the radiance of the Father's glory.

Together with the Spirit, the Father and Son move as one.

Healing the broken.
Freeing the oppressed.
Reconciling all things to Himself.

In Christ, we do not encounter a fragmented or distant God—but the fullness of the living God.

One in essence.
Infinite in love.
Overflowing with grace.
Undivided in power, mercy, and mission to redeem.

Why God's Oneness Cannot Be Broken

God's oneness means God is never divided.

His love, justice, holiness, and mercy aren't parts of who He is—they're the *fullness* of His being, always working in perfect harmony.

Unlike us, God is never in conflict with Himself.

His will, His actions, and His heart flow in perfect unity.

This matters deeply.

It means we cannot pit His justice against His love, or His holiness against His grace.

They are not opposites.

They are one.

To experience God's mercy is to encounter His holiness. To face His judgment is to stand in the presence of His love.

God doesn't shift roles.

He is *always* fully Himself—complete, whole, and unchanging.

If God were divided, He could be inconsistent.

But because He is one, He is always faithful, always true, and never changing:

> *The LORD is righteous in all His ways, and faithful in all His deeds.*
>
> *— Psalm 145:17*

How God's Oneness Transforms Your Life

Understanding God's oneness guards your heart.

Only the one true God deserves your worship—because only He is Creator, Sustainer, and Redeemer.

In a world of empty promises and endless distractions, His oneness calls you back to the center: **He alone is enough.**

> *Look to Me, and be saved, every part of the earth; for I am God, and there is no other.*
>
> *— Isaiah 45:22*

When this truth sinks in, it transforms everything:

Your worship becomes undivided—focused and free.

Your faith becomes unshakable—anchored in the eternal.

Your life becomes aligned—walking in rhythm with His will.

> **God's oneness doesn't just reveal who He is—it reshapes who you are.**

And when you see Him as He truly is, everything else fades.

The Danger of Misunderstanding God

An idol isn't always another god.

Sometimes, it's a distorted image of the true God.

Humanity was made in God's image—but Jesus is *the image of God* in whose likeness we were created.

> *Who* [the Son] *is the image of the invisible God.*
>
> — *Colossians 1:15*

> *He* [the Son] *is the radiance of His* [the Father's] *glory, the very image of His substance.*
>
> — *Hebrews 1:3*

Yet many people unknowingly hold a warped view—seeing the Father as distant, stern, or unapproachable, and Jesus as loving—but as if He's protecting us from the Father's wrath.

But this is not the Gospel as the Early Church understood it.

Jesus isn't saving us from the Father—He's revealing the Father.

Every healing.

Every word of grace.

Every act of compassion.

It was the Father's heart flowing through the Son.

> *Truly, I tell you, the Son can do nothing of Himself, but what He sees the Father doing.*
>
> — *John 5:19*

38

When Jesus knelt to defend the woman caught in adultery (John 8), it wasn't mercy versus justice.

It was the Father's justice and mercy working in perfect unity.

> **Jesus is the perfect Mediator—not because He protects us from the Father, but because He brings us to Him.**

To experience the Son's love is to encounter the love of the Father.

God Is Not Three Separate Beings

At the heart of the Christian faith is this unshakable truth: *God is one.*

This protects us from *tritheism*—the false belief that the Father, Son, and Spirit are three separate gods acting independently.

This misunderstanding breaks our worship, divides God's nature, and distorts our relationship with Him.

Is the Trinity Three Gods?

The Early Church rejected tritheism.

Yet today, many believers unknowingly drift toward this trap.

If we see the Father as *wrathful* and Jesus as *loving*, we fracture God's nature—imagining conflict where there is unity.

But Jesus said:

The Father judges no one, but He has given all judgment to the Son.

— John 5:22

The Father's justice is the Son's justice.

The Son's love is the Father's love.

They are one in will, in heart, and in purpose.

To divide God's attributes is to distort His nature—and to diminish the beauty of His oneness.

When we separate them, we misunderstand Him.

When we unite them, we see His glory.

The Trinity is not fragmented.

The Father, Son, and Spirit do not act in contradiction—what the Son reveals is exactly what the Father feels.

The Trinity is one God—perfectly united in essence, mission, and love.

Looking Ahead

We've stood at Sinai and reclaimed the blazing truth at the heart of biblical faith: God is one.

His love, justice, and holiness are not competing forces—they are the undivided essence of who He is.

But if God is so holy that no one can see His face and live... how can we draw near?

In the next chapter, we'll encounter the mystery of the Father—the unseen Source of all life, whose glory is veiled in light, yet whose heart longs to be known.

Reflection and Study Guide

Chapter 2: Worshiping the One True God

Hear, O Israel: The Lord our God, the Lord is one.
— Deuteronomy 6:4

Questions for Reflection

- **The Heart of Worship:** How does knowing that God is one—perfectly united in essence, purpose, and love—deepen your worship and strengthen your trust in Him?

- **Confronting Distortions:** Have you ever unintentionally divided God's character—assigning judgment to the Father and mercy to the Son? How does understanding God's unity challenge these misconceptions?

- **Trusting God's Unity:** In moments of uncertainty or brokenness, how does God's unchanging oneness strengthen your faith in His goodness and provision?

Key Takeaways

- **God's Indivisibility:** God is perfectly united in essence, purpose, and love. His love, justice, mercy, and power are not separate traits—they flow fully and inseparably from His being.

- **Rejecting Idolatry:** God's oneness calls us to forsake all idols—whether false images (for Christ alone is the image of God) or misplaced priorities—so we can offer Him undivided worship and allegiance.

- **Relational Oneness:** God's unity is not abstract but deeply relational—revealed through the Son, made present by the Spirit, and drawing us into eternal fellowship with the Father.

Practical Application

- **Meditate on the Shema:** Spend time each day reflecting on Deuteronomy 6:4–5. Let these words deepen your worship, reminding you that God is one and wholly deserving of your heart, soul, and strength.

- **Identify Hidden Idols:** Ask God to reveal any distorted views or misplaced trust that divide your heart. Confess and surrender these areas, inviting Him to realign your worship and life with His truth.

- **Worship in Unity:** In prayer and worship, thank God for the perfect unity of His work in creation, redemption, and restoration. Celebrate the harmony of the Father, Son, and Spirit—and trust Him to bring that same unity into every part of your life.

PART 2—KNOWING GOD

Father, Son, and Spirit Revealed

Chapter 3: God the Father—The Source of Life

The Father's Call

Have you ever felt a longing for love, belonging, and purpose—like something just beyond your reach?

What if that longing isn't random, but a whisper from the One who created you?

Look up.

Have you ever stood beneath a starlit sky, overwhelmed by its vastness, and felt something stir deep inside—an awe beyond words?

The same God who shaped every star and calls them by name—the Creator who spoke galaxies into existence—made you in His image.

You were created for His love—nothing else can satisfy.

When Jesus taught His disciples to pray, He began with these life-changing words:

> ***Our Father*** *in Heaven, holy be Your name.*
> *— Matthew 6:9*

These words reveal a truth that reshapes our entire understanding of God:

The Creator of the universe is not only infinite and all-powerful—He is deeply personal.

45

The same God who upholds the cosmos knows every hair on your head (Luke 12:7).

To call Him Father is to rest in the certainty that you are deeply loved, fully known, and never abandoned.

But it's more than just a title for prayer.

To call God Father redefines your identity, your purpose, and your place in the world.

It anchors your life in the truth of who He is—and who you are in Him.

Yet this truth also presents a paradox.

The Mystery of the Father's Nearness

God's holiness is absolute. His power is limitless.

Scripture declares He dwells in unapproachable light (1 Timothy 6:16), and that no one can see His face and live (Exodus 33:20).

His glory is too radiant, His purity too consuming, for sinful humanity to stand in the fullness of His presence.

And yet—He draws near.

How can a God so holy also be so personal?

This is the great mystery of the Father's love:

- He is enthroned in Heaven, yet *present* with the brokenhearted (Psalm 34:18).

- He is a consuming fire, yet a *refuge* for His children (Hebrews 12:29, Psalm 91:2).

- He is beyond all things, yet *closer* than our breath (Acts 17:28).

But how is this possible?

The answer is the Son.

As the Mediator, He bridges the gap—making a relationship with the Father not only possible, but deeply personal.

Through the Son, the Father's love is revealed.

By the Spirit, His presence becomes real in our lives.

The Trinity is an invitation into a love so vast and unshakable that it draws us into the very heart of the Father Himself.

Created for Love: The Father's Purpose

From the very first words of Scripture, the Father is revealed as the Creator of all things:

> *In the beginning God created the heavens and the earth.*
> *— Genesis 1:1*

This first verse unveils a breathtaking truth.

The Father is the source of all existence—the One from whom every atom, heartbeat, and galaxy springs to life.

Paul echoes this in the New Testament:

> *There is one God, the Father, from whom are all things, and we for Him.*
> *— 1 Corinthians 8:6*

Creation was no accident.

It wasn't born out of necessity.

It was an act of love.

Every sunrise, every star, every living thing reflects the Father's heart—revealing a God who sustains creation with care and purpose.

And yet, His transcendence must not be overlooked.
He is infinitely greater than creation itself:

> *Look, Heaven and the highest Heaven can't contain You.*
> *— 2 Chronicles 6:18*

The Father's Glory: Holy Yet Near

To grasp this mystery, imagine the sun.
Its warmth gives life to the earth.
Without it, nothing could survive.
But if the sun itself appeared in your living room, its intensity would consume everything.
In the same way, Scripture describes the Father's holiness:

> *Our God is a consuming fire.*
> *— Hebrews 12:29*

The Father's presence is pure, radiant, and beyond human comprehension.
His holiness is not just an attribute—it is the very essence of who He is.
And yet—He does not remain distant.
While His glory is overwhelming, His love is even greater.
This is why Scripture says:

> *The fear of the LORD is the beginning of wisdom.*
> *— Proverbs 9:10*

The Hebrew word for fear (*yirah*) points to an awe-filled reverence—a recognition that we stand before a God of absolute majesty.

Yet the same God also declares:

> *There is no fear [phobos: terror, alarm] in love; but perfect love casts out fear.*
> — *1 John 4:18*

This is the paradox of the Father's nature:

- His holiness inspires reverence, yet His love invites intimacy.
- His greatness fills us with awe, yet His kindness draws us close.

The One who spoke galaxies into being calls you His child —drawing you near not as a distant Creator, but as *Abba*, your loving Heavenly Father.

Why No One Can See the Father's Glory

God's glory is beyond human comprehension.
He's not just greater than creation—He is utterly set apart:

> *Who alone has immortality, dwelling in unapproachable light; whom no human has seen, nor can see.*
> — *1 Timothy 6:16*

When Moses asked to see His glory, God replied:

> *You cannot see My face, for man may not see Me and live.*
> — *Exodus 33:20*

This truth runs throughout Scripture:

- When Isaiah saw a vision of the Lord, he cried out: *Woe is me. For I am undone* (Isaiah 6:5).
- When God's presence rested on Mount Sinai, the Israelites trembled and begged Moses to speak to God on their behalf (Exodus 20:18–19).
- Even the ark of the covenant—symbolizing God's presence—was untouchable. When Uzzah reached out to steady it, he perished instantly (2 Samuel 6:6–7).

This is the weight of God's transcendence—His holiness is so radiant, so pure, that no sinful being can stand in the fullness of His majesty.

But this raises an important question.

If the Father longs for relationship with us, why is His majesty hidden from our sight?

The answer is love.

The veil of His glory is not a barrier meant to keep us away —it is a mercy that protects us.

Like the sun's intensity, His transcendent glory is too overwhelming for us to bear in our current state.

If we beheld Him fully, we would be consumed.

The Unseen Glory of the Father

Throughout history, the Father's presence was always *shielded*—not because He was distant, but because His holiness was absolute.

In the temple, a veil separated the Holy of Holies—where God's presence dwelled—from the rest of the people.

Only the high priest could enter, once a year, on the Day of Atonement—and only with blood to cover sin.

Bells were sewn onto his robe, and a rope tied around his waist—so if he entered unclean and died, no one would risk stepping inside.

This wasn't because God was cruel.

It was because sin cannot survive in His absolute fullness.

But at the cross, everything changed.

When Jesus died, the temple veil was torn from top to bottom—not by human hands, but by the power of God:

> *And look, the curtain of the temple was torn in two from the top to the bottom.*
> *— Matthew 27:51*

Through Christ, the *barrier* was removed.

Through Christ, we now have *access* to the Father.

> *Let us therefore draw near with boldness to the throne of grace, that we may receive mercy, and may find grace for help in time of need.*
> *— Hebrews 4:16*

Through the Spirit, we have real and intimate access to the Father—heart to heart, spirit to Spirit.

Yet our mortal bodies are not yet ready to stand before His unveiled majesty.

So even now, the fullness of the Father's glory remains veiled in unapproachable light (1 Timothy 6:16).

But one day, even that final barrier will be lifted (Philippians 3:21).

We will see Him face-to-face—no veil remaining, no separation left.

Until then, Jesus remains our Mediator (1 Timothy 2:5)—bridging Heaven and earth, Spirit and flesh—so that even now, we can draw near in boldness...and one day, in glory.

One Day, You Will See the Father

The book of Revelation paints a stunning picture of the future—when the new heaven and new earth are revealed, and God becomes all in all (1 Corinthians 15:28).

On that day, the Father will no longer remain veiled.

> *Look, the tabernacle of God is with humans, and He will dwell with them.*
>
> — *Revelation 21:3*

For the first time, creation will behold the Father's face:

> *They will see His face.*
>
> — *Revelation 22:4*

In that moment, *all* barriers will be gone.

Sin will be no more.

The fire of His holiness will no longer consume—it will ignite everlasting joy.

This is the Father's ultimate purpose—not to remain hidden, but to restore all things so that we may dwell with Him forever.

The Father's Plan: Restoring Everything

The Father's love is the driving force behind His plan to redeem and restore everything sin has broken.

Salvation begins and ends with the Father's heart.

Long before humanity knew its need for redemption, the Father had already set His plan in motion—preparing the way for a face-to-face encounter with Himself.

How the Father's Love Gave Us Jesus

> *The God and Father of our Lord Jesus Christ... chose us in Him **before** the foundation of the world.*
>
> *— Ephesians 1:3–4*

The Father's plan of salvation was not a reaction to sin—it was eternal. Before creation itself, He had *already* determined to draw us into the fullness of His love, presence, and purpose.

From beginning to end, redemption is the Father's design.

> *For this is how God* [the Father] *loved the world: He gave His only Son.*
>
> *— John 3:16*

Jesus affirmed this when He said:

> *For I have come down from Heaven, not to do My own will, but the will of Him who sent Me.*
>
> *— John 6:38*

The Father is the architect of salvation.
He is actively working through the Son, as Jesus declared:

> *The Father who lives in Me does His works.*
> — *John 14:10*

Paul echoed this truth:

> God [the Father] *was in Christ reconciling the world to Himself.*
> — *2 Corinthians 5:19*

How the Father Is Drawing You Closer

The Father's role in salvation has not ended.
Even now, He is the One drawing people to Himself.
That unshakable longing stirring inside you?
It's the Father calling you.
The awe you feel when you look at creation?
It's His voice, inviting you nearer.
Even when we turn away, He never stops pursuing us:

> *No one can come to Me unless the Father who sent Me draws him.*
> — *John 6:44*

The Father is not a distant figure in salvation.
He is its source, its architect, and its unstoppable force of love.

The Father's Love: Deeper Than You Ever Imagined

The Father's saving plan reveals the breathtaking depth of His love—a love so vast it cannot be measured.

Salvation is not merely an act of mercy. It is the overflow of His infinite love, spanning the divide of sin to bring us home.

The Father's love has always been pursuing you.

Before you took your first breath, before you knew your need for Him—He had *already* set His love upon you.

The cross wasn't a last-minute rescue mission.

It was the Father's plan before time began (Ephesians 1:3–4).

The Father's Love Is Our Ultimate Home

The grand story of Scripture reveals a stunning truth:

The Father's greatest desire is to dwell with His people.

From the very beginning, His plan has been to bring us into His presence—not as distant worshipers, but as His beloved children.

As Paul declared:

> *For of Him, and through Him, and to Him, are all things: to whom be glory for ever. Amen.*
>
> *— Romans 11:36, KJV*

Heaven isn't about golden streets or pearly gates.

It's about being with the Father.

The One who spoke galaxies into existence calls you His child.

He is not distant or indifferent—*He is Abba.*

And He invites you into His eternal embrace.

The Father's transcendence stirs reverence.

But His love invites intimacy.

This is the mystery of the Father:

He is infinitely holy—yet He draws near to make you His own.

Looking Ahead

We've stood in awe of the Father—holy, unseen, and yet full of love.

The Source of all life, whose glory no one can behold, yet whose heart longs to draw us near.

But how does such a God reveal Himself without consuming us?

In the next chapter, we'll encounter the eternal Word—the visible image of the invisible God—who appeared in fire, in whispers, and ultimately...in flesh.

Not a second deity, but the Father's own self-expression—who became the Son for our redemption.

Get ready to see how the God no one could see became the Savior everyone could follow.

Reflection and Study Guide

Chapter 3: God the Father—The Source of Life

There is one God, the Father, from whom are all things, and we for Him. — 1 Corinthians 8:6

Questions for Reflection

- **The Father's Call:** How does knowing the Father's love—as both your Creator and Abba—reshape your identity and purpose?

- **God's Transcendence:** How does recognizing the Father's unapproachable holiness deepen your awe of His greatness while increasing your gratitude for His love?

- **The Goal of Creation:** How does knowing that the Father's ultimate plan is to dwell with His glorified creation fill you with hope for the future?

Key Takeaways

- **The Father's Love and Transcendence:** The Father is both infinitely transcendent and deeply personal. His glory fills the heavens, yet He invites you to know Him as Abba.

- **The Father's Saving Plan:** The Father's plan of salvation was not a reaction to sin but an eternal design. Through the Son and Spirit, He works to bring humanity into His presence.

- **The Father's Ultimate Goal:** The Father's desire is to glorify creation and dwell with His people. Heaven is defined not by its splendor but by the Father's presence.

Practical Application

- **Meditate on God's Holiness:** This week, spend time reflecting on the Father's transcendence by meditating on Scriptures like Exodus 33:20 and 1 Timothy 6:16. Let His holiness stir awe and deepen reverence in your heart.

- **Draw Near in Worship:** In light of the Father's love, set aside time to worship Him as both Creator and Abba. Thank Him for revealing His heart through creation, the Son, and the Spirit.

- **Live in the Father's Love:** Embrace the truth that you are fully known and fully loved by your Heavenly Father. Let His love transform how you live, love, and worship each day.

Chapter 4: Jesus Christ—God's Visible Image

The Question That Changes Everything

Who is Jesus?

No question has shaped history, redefined faith, or transformed lives more than this.

Understanding Jesus' divinity means recognizing His distinction without dividing God's oneness, and embracing the Father-Son relationship at the heart of the Gospel.

For centuries, believers have sought a one-size-fits-all answer. But rather than offering a simple definition, the Bible reveals a living narrative—the story of God's visible image—often hidden beneath layers of theology.

Throughout history, different perspectives have sought to explain Jesus' identity:

- **Arianism** emphasized Christ's distinction so strongly that it ultimately denied His divinity.

- **Modalism** affirmed God's oneness but treated the Father, Son, and Spirit as different "modes"—losing the genuine relational connection revealed in the Gospels.

- **Traditional Trinitarianism** upheld both oneness and distinction, yet often presented the Old and New Testaments as if God's self-revelation had *always* been fully expressed—rather than gradually unfolding.

Each view captured part of the truth but struggled to embrace the whole picture.

So how do we hold both truths together?

By allowing Scripture to reveal the Son's identity as it unfolds—starting in the Old Testament and culminating in the New.

Throughout Scripture, God's self-revelation follows a consistent pattern:

The Father as the unseen source.
The Word as His visible expression.
The Spirit as His power moving through His Word.

This pattern runs throughout the Old Testament, yet it's not until the Incarnation that we find the Father-Son relationship *fully* emerge.

Step by step, God revealed Himself through His Word—first through appearances, then through prophecy, and ultimately, in the flesh.

Throughout the Old Testament, God's Word appeared as His visible presence—preparing the way for the ultimate moment: *The Word becoming flesh and walking among us.*

This chapter traces the Word's journey from eternity to Bethlehem, showing how God's visible image took on flesh, became the Son, and fully revealed the Father's heart at the center of the Gospel.

How the Father Reveals Himself

Imagine building a vast, living world—like a real-life video game or virtual reality—where every character has a story, and every choice matters.

Though you fill the world with beauty, you yourself exist beyond its limits—unseen and untouchable.

People experience what you've made—but can't see you.

How could you make yourself known?

The only way would be to step into their world—taking on a form they could see, hear, and touch.

The Bible declares that God is so holy, so transcendent, that no one can see Him and live (Exodus 33:20).

And yet, throughout the Old Testament, something astonishing happens—**people see God.**

Abraham welcomes Him as a guest (Genesis 18:1–3).

Jacob wrestles with Him in the night (Genesis 32:24–30).

Moses speaks with Him face-to-face (Exodus 33:11).

Clearly, God's visible presence was active long before Bethlehem.

How can both be true?

The answer lies in *the Word*.

The Word of the Lord was the means by which the transcendent Father made Himself known without overwhelming creation with His full glory.

The Word Existed Before Jesus Was Born

Before Bethlehem, God the Son was not yet revealed—but the Word of the Lord was *already* present—God's active, visible self-expression in creation.

At the Incarnation, the eternal Word entered time, taking on human flesh and becoming the man Jesus.

But even before Jesus' earthly life, the Word of the Lord moved in the world, revealing God's presence and power.

John connects Jesus directly to this living Word:

> *In the beginning was the Word, and the Word was with God, and the Word was God. He was in the beginning with God. All things were made through Him, and apart from Him nothing was made that has been made. In Him was life, and the life was the light of humanity.*
>
> — *John 1:1–4*

John reveals profound truths about the Word:

- **The Word is *with* God** — showing distinction from the Father.
- **The Word *was* God** — affirming His full divinity.
- **The Word is the agent of creation** — all things were made through Him.
- **In Him is life and light** — the revelation of the Father's heart.

The Word is not a separate deity but the Father's self-revealing expression—His visible, active presence in creation.

When the Word Became the Son

Many assume Jesus has always been the Son—*eternally begotten*, forever existing in a Father-Son relationship.

But Scripture never speaks of an "eternal Son."

Instead, it shows the Son revealed in time, through the Incarnation, and for redemption.

The Word became flesh and lived among us, and we saw His glory, such glory as of the one and only of the Father, full of grace and truth.

— John 1:14

Before the Incarnation, the Son *was* the Word.
At the Incarnation, the Word *became* the Son.
Paul echoes this:

But when the fullness of the time came, God sent out His Son, born to a woman.

— Galatians 4:4

The Son is sent *in time*, not eternally co-existing in personal distinction from the Father.

His Sonship is revealed progressively—through:

- **Incarnation** — taking on a human soul and body.
- **Submission** — learning obedience in suffering (Hebrews 5:8).
- **Glorification** — being exalted and enthroned (Philippians 2:6–11).

The Son is not a second divine person who eternally existed in the same way as the Father—He is the eternal Word, proceeding from the Father, who became human and, in doing so, entered into a real, living Father-Son relationship.

When He brings in the Firstborn into the world He says, "Let all the angels of God worship Him."

— Hebrews 1:6

63

If the Son were eternally distinct, why does Scripture tie His worship to His arrival? Why does every knee bow to Him *because* of His obedience (Philippians 2:8–10)? Why is He declared worthy *because* He was slain (Revelation 5:9)?

The Son was not eternally begotten. His personal distinction as the Son began through the Incarnation—yet the eternal Word was *always* fully divine and uncreated.

This doesn't diminish Christ's divinity—it magnifies the miracle of the Incarnation.

Concept	Eternal Word (Logos)	Incarnate Son (Jesus)
Present in Creation?	Yes	Not yet born
Personally Distinct?	Functionally distinct	Personally distinct
Called "Son of God"?	No	Yes
Shares God's Nature?	Fully divine	Fully God & fully man
Begotten?	Not begotten	Begotten

Even Tertullian, an Early Church theologian writing in the second century, saw God's relational roles unfolding in time:

> *God is in like manner a Father, and He is also a Judge; but He has not always been Father and Judge... There was, however, a time when neither sin existed with Him, nor the Son... How neatly does Scripture lend us its aid, when it applies the two titles to Him with a distinction, and reveals them each at its proper time!*
>
> — Tertullian, *Against Hermogenes*, Chapter 3

This distinction—between the *eternal Word* and the *incarnate Son*—unlocks a deeper understanding of the Old Testament appearances of God.

The Word in the Old Testament

The Word of the Lord was more than speech—it was the Father's visible, active self-revelation.

The Word Appeared to Abraham

> *After these things the Word of the LORD came to Abram in a vision, saying, "Do not be afraid, Abram. **I am your shield**... **I am God**, who brought you out of Ur Kasdim to give you this land to possess."*
>
> *— Genesis 15:1–7*

Abraham didn't just hear God's voice—*he saw the Word* appear in a vision and declare Himself to be God.

The Word Appeared to Samuel

> *The Word of the LORD was rare in those days; there was no frequent vision... And the LORD came and stood, and called as at other times.*
>
> *— 1 Samuel 3:1–10*

In Samuel's day, visions were rare.

Yet one night, the Word of the Lord came, stood before Samuel, and called him by name.

The Word was not just heard—*He was seen.*

The Word Appeared to Jeremiah

> *Now the Word of the LORD came to me, saying, "Before I formed you in the belly, I knew you. Before you came forth out of the womb, I sanctified you. I have appointed you a prophet to the nations." Then I said, "Ah, Lord GOD. Look, I do not know how to speak; for I am a child."*
>
> *— Jeremiah 1:4–6*

Jeremiah didn't just receive a message—he encountered the living self-expression of God.

He recognized the One speaking to him as the Lord God—the personal name of *Yahweh Himself.*

In every case, the Word of the Lord was not merely a voice but the Father's **shielded** visible presence.

God's Wisdom in the Old Testament

In Scripture, Wisdom is not just an idea.

> *The LORD created Me in the beginning of His way, before His works of old. I was set up from everlasting... Before the earth existed. When there were no depths, I was brought forth... When He established the heavens, I was there... I was the craftsman by His side... Whoever finds Me finds life, and will obtain favor from the LORD.*
>
> *— Proverbs 8:22–30*

From the earliest times, both Jewish and Christian scholars recognized that Wisdom was more than a trait—it was God's own presence, personified in action.

Both Wisdom and the Word reveal the same breathtaking reality: God's life and light reaching into creation, making the Father known, and preparing the way for a more perfect unveiling in Christ.

The parallels between Wisdom in Proverbs and the Word in John's Gospel are unmistakable:

Word (John 1)	Wisdom (Proverbs 8)
Existed in the beginning (1:1).	Existed in the beginning (8:22).
With God (1:1).	By His side (8:30).
All things made through Him (1:3).	Craftsman at creation (8:30).
In Him was life (1:4).	Whoever finds me finds life (8:35).
Full of grace and truth (1:14).	Whose mouth speaks truth (8:7).
The Word became flesh (1:14).	Cries out in the streets (8:1–3).

John calls God's self-revelation the **Word** (*Logos*).

Proverbs calls it **Wisdom** (*Chokmah*).

Both are God's eternal self-expression—the life, light, and truth of the Father revealed to creation.

Paul leaves no doubt when he writes:

> *Christ is the power of God and the Wisdom of God.*
> — *1 Corinthians 1:24*

Long before Bethlehem, the eternal Word was revealing the Father's heart and shaping the universe.

The Angel of the Lord

Throughout the Old Testament, another striking figure emerges—the Angel of the Lord.

Unlike created angels, this Messenger:

- Speaks as God.
- Forgives sins.
- Receives worship—acts reserved for God alone.

This Angel was not a created being, but a dynamic manifestation of the Father's presence—appearing in tangible form within creation.

Each of these expressions—the Angel, the Word, and Wisdom—fulfills the same divine role: delivering truth, revealing the Father's heart, and carrying out His will.

The Angel Appeared to Moses

> *The Angel of the LORD appeared to him in a flame of fire out of the midst of a bush... God called to him out of the midst of the bush... "I am the God of your fathers, the God of Abraham, and the God of Isaac, and the God of Jacob." Moses hid his face; for he was afraid to look at God.*
>
> — *Exodus 3:2–6*

At first, He is called the Angel of the LORD.

Moments later, He declares, *I am the God of your fathers.*

This is no ordinary angel.

This is God appearing in visible form.

The Angel Appeared to Gideon and Is Worshiped

> *The Angel of the LORD appeared to him, and said to him, "The LORD is with you, mighty warrior..." Gideon saw that he was the Angel of the LORD; and Gideon said, "Alas, Lord GOD. Because I have seen the Angel of the LORD face to face." The LORD said to him, "Peace be to you. Do not be afraid. You shall not die."*
>
> *— Judges 6:12–23*

At first, Gideon thinks he is speaking to a messenger.

But when he realizes *he has seen God*, he is filled with fear.

Unlike created angels, this figure receives worship and speaks with divine authority.

The Angel Wrestles with Jacob

> *So Jacob called the name of the place Peniel: "For I have seen God face to face, and my life has been preserved."*
>
> *— Genesis 32:30*

Jacob wrestles with a man—but afterward declares: *I have seen God face to face.*

Again, a physical encounter with God—yet shielded from the Father's full, unapproachable glory.

Each appearance pointing to the ultimate moment:

When God would not just *appear*—but fully become one of us.

The same divine Messenger who spoke to Abraham, Moses, and Gideon would one day walk among us as Jesus Christ.

Jesus: The Image of the Invisible God

The Old Testament presents a mystery fulfilled in Christ: God is invisible and unapproachable—yet people saw Him and lived. Like a game creator stepping into their own world, He made Himself visible so we could know the One who made us.

The New Testament resolves the mystery:

> *No one has seen God* [the Father] *at any time. The only Son* [the Word], *who is at the Father's side, has made Him known.*
>
> — *John 1:18*

The Word is the bridge between unseen glory and revealed presence.

Scripture foretold that the One who appeared as God's visible image would one day become flesh:

> *I will raise up your descendant after you... and I will establish His throne forever. **I will be His Father**, and He shall be My Son.*
>
> — *2 Samuel 7:12–14*

> *For to us **a Child is born**. To us a Son is given; and the government will be on His shoulders, and His name is called Wonderful Counselor, Mighty God, Everlasting Father.*
>
> — *Isaiah 9:6*

> *You are My Son. Today I have **become** Your Father.*
>
> — *Psalm 2:7*

These prophecies pointed to a coming shift: from appearances to *Incarnation*—from self-revelation to *Sonship*.

The Word Became Flesh

The Word became flesh and lived among us.
— *John 1:14*

The Word didn't simply inhabit a body—He became fully human, fully God and fully man.

What distinguished Him from the Father was not a separate divine essence, but His real, embodied humanity:

- **A physical body**, capable of hunger, fatigue, and death.
- **A human soul**, capable of sorrow, learning, and obedience.

Though sinless, His flesh was subject to weakness (Romans 8:3). He felt the natural pull of human instincts—the drive toward self-preservation, the real weight of suffering.

Yet at every moment, He brought the desires of His flesh into perfect submission to the will of the Father.

Thus He prayed:

Not My will [the desire of My flesh], *but Yours* [the desire of My Spirit], *be done.*
— *Luke 22:42*

Here, the Father-Son relationship moves from mystery into full view.

71

The Word who once spoke *as* the Father now speaks *for* the Father—out of a real human life, fully surrendered in perfect love.

Rather than dividing God, the Incarnation pulls back the veil, revealing the Father's heart more fully than ever before.

The fullness of the Father dwells bodily in Christ (Colossians 2:9), bridging Heaven and earth.

God the Father remains the unseen source, while the Word becomes truly human (God the Son)—distinct in the flesh, yet perfectly one with the Father in Spirit.

Looking Ahead

We've followed the eternal Word from creation to Incarnation—the visible image of the invisible God, stepping into history not as a second deity, but as the Father's own self-expression made flesh.

In Jesus, the fullness of God shines in human form—not just to reveal the Father, but also to reveal us.

He came to show what it truly means to live fully alive in the Spirit.

In the next chapter, we'll discover how Jesus models the life we were created for—a life not powered by divine privilege, but marked by prayer, surrender, and Spirit-filled obedience.

We'll see how the One who reveals God also reveals you.

Reflection and Study Guide

Chapter 4: Jesus Christ—God's Visible Image

Who is the image of the invisible God, the Firstborn over all creation. — Colossians 1:15

Questions for Reflection

- **The Son in the Old Testament:** How does seeing Jesus as the Word of the Lord, the Angel of the Lord, and Divine Wisdom deepen your understanding of His role in God's self-revelation?

- **Progressive Revelation:** The Father-Son relationship was hinted at in the Old Testament but fully revealed through the Incarnation. How does this shape your view of the Bible as one unified story?

- **God Made Known:** How does knowing Jesus as the visible image of the Father transform the way you approach prayer, worship, and daily life?

Key Takeaways

- **Jesus as the Father's Visible Presence:** The Word and the Angel of the Lord were not created beings but were God's visible, active presence revealing the Father before the Incarnation.

- **From Presence to Person:** In the Old Testament, the Word was God's visible expression; through the Incarnation, the Word took on full human personhood, revealing a real and relational Father-Son distinction.

- **God's Revelation Unfolds:** The Father did not change; rather, His self-revelation unfolded over time, culminating in the Word becoming flesh.

Practical Application

- **Read and Reflect:** Read Psalm 33:6, Genesis 15:1–6, 1 Samuel 3:1–10, Jeremiah 1:4–10, and John 1:1–14. Journal how these passages reveal God's unfolding self-revelation over time.

- **Pray with Confidence:** Since Jesus fully reveals the Father, approach God in prayer with boldness, knowing He is near and intimately present.

- **Live Daily in the Incarnation:** Jesus remains forever the Son of God and Son of Man. How can you cultivate a daily awareness of His living presence in your everyday life?

Chapter 5: Jesus Our Model and Mediator

Jesus: Revealing God and Revealing You

What if Jesus not only revealed God—but also revealed your true identity?

Many recognize that Jesus came to reveal the Father, but fewer realize a profound truth:

Jesus didn't just come to reveal God—*He came to reveal us*—humanity fully alive in the Spirit.

When Jesus walked the earth, He wasn't just God among men—He was also fully human, living in perfect union with the Father.

He didn't come just to stand apart—*but to restore us*, revealing the Father's heart and the life we were created for.

This leads to some of the most important and personal questions about Jesus:

If Jesus is fully God, why did He need to pray?

If He is all-knowing, how could He grow in wisdom?

If He is one with the Father, why did He say, *The Father is greater than I?*

Answering these questions doesn't just deepen our understanding of Jesus—it reveals something even more personal: *our true identity.*

75

In Christ's humanity, we find the divine pattern we were created to follow.

As a man, Jesus didn't live from divine advantage but from divine alignment.

This alignment was a divine flow—from the Father, through the Son (the Word), and by the Spirit.

But Jesus' life—His Baptism, death, Resurrection, and Ascension—didn't just transform His humanity; it opened the door for all who are united to Him to walk in this same divine relationship.

Understanding the Divine Pattern

Throughout the Old Testament, the Spirit of God always moved through the Word of God.

- The **Word** of the Lord spoke creation into existence, and the *Spirit* manifested that Word (Genesis 1:1–3).
- The **Word** came to the prophets, and the *Spirit* carried them along to speak (2 Peter 1:21).
- The **Angel** of the Lord (the Word) appeared to Gideon, and the *Spirit* came upon him to lead (Judges 6:12, 6:34).

The Spirit never acted independently, but always flowed from the Father, through the Word, and into creation.

This divine flow continued through every generation—until one final prophet appeared, standing on the threshold of something entirely new.

John the Baptist: The Final Old Testament Prophet

John the Baptist was the last prophet of the Old Covenant —the promised "Elijah" who would prepare the way for the Messiah (Malachi 4:5).

> *Among those who are born of women there has not arisen anyone greater than John the Baptist; yet he who is least in the Kingdom of Heaven is greater than he.*
> *— Matthew 11:11*

John was uniquely set apart, filled with the Spirit from the womb (Luke 1:15).

Yet even he did not carry the *fullness* of the Spirit.

His role was not to complete God's revelation, but to prepare the way for the One who would.

Before Jesus, the Spirit had been given only in part—never in fullness.

Until now, the Word revealed the Father from *outside* human nature.

But everything was about to change.

The Word *became* flesh, paving the way for the Spirit to *indwell* humanity *permanently*.

Why Jesus' Baptism Changed Everything

When Jesus stepped into the Jordan to be baptized, something unprecedented occurred:

> *The heavens were opened to Him, and He saw the Spirit of God descending as a dove, and coming on Him. And look, a*

> *voice out of the heavens said, "This is My beloved Son, with whom I am well pleased."*
>
> — *Matthew 3:16–17*

This was not just another moment of the Spirit anointing a prophet.

It was the moment when the fullness of God's Spirit was poured into human nature—*without measure.*

> *He whom God has sent speaks the words of God; for He does not give the Spirit by measure.*
>
> — *John 3:34*

For the first time, the divine pattern was fully realized *inside* a human being!

The Spirit always moved in the same divine flow—from the Father, through His Word, and onto chosen vessels.

But now the Word Himself was flesh.

At Jesus' Baptism, the *fullness* of God's Spirit came to rest and reside in Christ alone.

> *For in Him all the fullness of Deity dwells in bodily form.*
>
> — *Colossians 2:9*

This explains why John's ministry began to decrease after this moment—the Old Covenant pattern had ended. The Spirit's activity was now concentrated entirely in Christ Jesus.

Jesus was not merely another anointed one—He was *the* Anointed One.

The vessel of divine fullness.

The fountain of life.

And now, the Spirit would be given through Him alone, filling and empowering all who are united to Him (John 16:7).

What the Incarnation Did *Not* Do

What exactly happened when the Word became flesh?

Did the eternal Word take over a human body?
Did a divine person merge with a human soul?
Or did something far more beautiful take place?

This is where the deepest confusion about the Trinity begins—but it's also where Scripture offers its most profound clarity.

Traditional Trinitarian theology has preserved essential truths, but in defending those truths, it leaned heavily on Greek philosophy, which Scripture never required.

As we explored in Chapter 1, thinkers like Plato defined "perfection" as static—timeless, changeless, and unmoved. Within that framework, saying the "eternal Son" *became something new*—fully human—introduces a contradiction the Church has long struggled to resolve.

In trying to preserve both Christ's divinity and humanity, the traditional model—supported by philosophy—collapses logically, unintentionally dividing Jesus into two selves:

1. **A divine self**—complete with a divine mind and will—who always existed, distinct from the Father,

2. **and a human self**—complete with a human mind and will—who comes into existence at the Incarnation.

But that's not one person—that's two.

Not *the Word became flesh*—but a merger of two persons.

And that's exactly what the Early Church condemned as *Nestorianism*—the heresy that split Christ into two separate individuals: one divine, one human.

To avoid this, some claimed the Word only took on a human body—not a full human soul.

But that leads to *Apollinarianism*—the heresy that said Jesus wasn't fully human at all, just God wrapped in flesh.

And the implications don't stop there.

If a divine person in the Trinity truly *changes* by taking on humanity, then the Trinity has changed.

But if God changes, even once, He's no longer unchanging—and the whole Gospel begins to unravel.

So tradition often replies: "This is a mystery."

But mystery is not a license for contradiction.

And Scripture never asks us to surrender reason in order to preserve tradition.

Thankfully, what tradition has made confusing, the Bible makes clear—and wonderfully beautiful.

The Word *became* flesh—not by fusing with another person, but by becoming a full and complete human life: spirit, soul, and body (John 1:14).

The Word was never one divine person alongside another. He was—and is—the Father's self-expression, now revealed in the person of Jesus Christ.

In the Incarnation, God didn't join Himself to a person.

He became a person.

He didn't send a representative. He didn't rent a body.

Through His eternal Word, the Father entered our world, generating—not adopting—a real human soul, personally distinct, yet bearing His exact image (Hebrews 1:3).

This is what Scripture calls: *the Son of God.*

The Word's personal distinction as the Son began at the Incarnation.

> **The Father's self-expression became flesh, and that human life became the bridge between Heaven and earth.**

This is not just theological clarity.

It's the breathtaking beauty of divine love.

The One who once dwelled in unapproachable light came close. He stepped into our weakness—not as a theory, but as *God with us* (Matthew 1:23).

That's why Jesus can be called "Everlasting Father" (Isaiah 9:6): so we could know the Father—made visible in the Son.

> *Philip said to Him, "Lord, show us the Father, and that will be enough for us." Jesus said to him, "Have I been with you all this time, and still you do not know Me, Philip? He who has seen Me has seen the Father. How can you say, 'Show us the Father?'"*
>
> *— John 14:8–9*

As we saw in the last chapter, Tertullian—writing long before Greek metaphysics (like timeless perfection) were imposed on the Trinity—affirmed that God was not always "Father," and that "the Son" was revealed in time, not eternity.

Scripture, he said, "applies the title...at its *proper time.*"

He wasn't speculating—he was helping the Church see

what Scripture had revealed all along.

This one shift resolves all the philosophical tensions that have clouded the Trinity for centuries. (*For a full comparison of these tensions and how this model answers them, see Appendix A*).

It stands in sharp contrast to the later doctrine that assumes—or insists—that the Son always existed as a distinct divine person, already living in a Father-Son relationship before becoming human.

In Christ, the fullness of God is revealed—not as a contradiction, but as the unfolding of divine love in human form.

If Jesus Is God, Why Did He Pray?

When the Word of the Lord became flesh, He didn't just inhabit a body—He fully embraced the human experience, including its limitations.

Remember, Jesus didn't live from divine advantage but from divine alignment:

> *Who, being in the form of God, thought it not robbery to be equal with God: But made Himself of no reputation, and took upon Him the form of a servant, and was made in the likeness of men.*
>
> — *Philippians 2:6–7, KJV*

Jesus lived the same way you and I are called to live—in complete dependence on the Father.

That's what makes His prayer life so significant.

Through prayer, Jesus brought His human nature into perfect alignment with the Spirit.

Though His soul—the seat of His identity and awareness—was the exact imprint of the Father's nature (Hebrews 1:3), His flesh still bore the natural pull of human instincts: hunger, fatigue, and the impulse to avoid pain.

This is why He agonized in Gethsemane.

His struggle wasn't between two opposing wills—after all, Jesus and the Father are one (John 10:30).

It was the Spirit contending with the natural resistance of the flesh.

As Paul described:

> *For the flesh lusts against the Spirit, and the Spirit against the flesh; and these are contrary to one another.*
>
> *— Galatians 5:17*

Like us, Jesus' flesh recoiled at suffering. Yet His soul—fully united with the Father—remained steadfast:

> *For we do not have a High Priest who cannot be touched with the feeling of our infirmities, but One who has been in all points tempted like we are, yet without sin.*
>
> *— Hebrews 4:15*

In addition, Jesus possessed a human mind that needed to grow in wisdom (Luke 2:52).

Yet through prayer, He drew from the Spirit within, allowing divine wisdom to shape His human understanding.

Jesus lived the life we were created for—*fully* human, *fully* dependent on God.

And this is exactly how it works for us today:

We have the Spirit of Christ within us (Romans 8:9–11)—yet we still wrestle with the pull of the flesh.

We have the mind of Christ (1 Corinthians 2:16)—yet we must grow into spiritual maturity.

We are seated with Christ in heavenly places (Ephesians 2:6)—yet we still navigate the challenges of earthly life.

This is why Jesus prayed. And why we should too.

Prayer wasn't a concession to weakness.

It was the wellspring of His strength—revealing the power of a human life *fully* surrendered to the Spirit of God.

If the Son of God depended on prayer as a man, how much more must we?

This same dependence is what He meant when He said, *The Father is greater than I.*

The Father Is Greater Than I

If Jesus is fully God, how can the Father be greater?

The answer lies in Jesus' humanity.

At first glance, His words—*The Father is greater than I* (John 14:28)—seem to challenge His divinity.

But Jesus wasn't speaking of His divine nature.

He was describing His humbled role in the Incarnation—living in full dependence on the Father as the model of Spirit-filled humanity.

As the Word made flesh, He embraced human limitation, becoming the example of perfect dependence on the Father.

In this role, He received everything from the Father:

- **Authority** — *All authority has been given to Me in Heaven and on earth* (Matthew 28:18).

- **Life** — *For as the Father has life in Himself, even so He gave to the Son also to have life in Himself* (John 5:26).

- **Judgment** — *For the Father judges no one, but He has given all judgment to the Son* (John 5:22).

That's what Jesus meant—not a denial of His divinity, but a display of human dependence.

The Divine Pattern Remains

What's incredible is that the Trinity's divine pattern didn't stop with Jesus—*it now flows through us*, drawing us into the life of God.

Just as Jesus received from the Father, we are now called to receive from Him:

- Jesus, who received all divine authority, *now shares that authority with us in His name* (Luke 10:19).

- Jesus, filled with the Holy Spirit, *now pours out His Spirit upon us* (Acts 2:33).

- Jesus, the Firstborn Son, *now makes us sons and daughters of God* (Romans 8:29).

The Word took on human flesh so He could bring us into the same relationship He has with the Father.

As He is, so are we in this world.

— 1 John 4:17

What Jesus' Ascension Means for Us

After His Resurrection, Jesus didn't simply return to Heaven and step away—He ascended to the Father's right hand, where He now reigns as both *God and man*, forever bridging Heaven and earth.

His Ascension wasn't about leaving us behind.

It was about bringing us into His victory and releasing His Spirit into our hearts.

God never wanted just one Son—He wanted a family.

> *For whom He foreknew, He also predestined to be conformed to the image of His Son, that He might be the Firstborn among many brothers.*
>
> *— Romans 8:29*

Jesus didn't just save us from sin—*He transformed us.*

He conquered sin so we could walk in freedom.

He defeated death so we could live with eternal purpose.

He ascended so we could reign with Him.

> *He who believes in Me, the works that I do, he will do also; and he will do greater works than these, because I am going to the Father.*
>
> *— John 14:12*

Jesus' Ascension wasn't the end—it was the ignition of a new era.

Through His Spirit, He now moves in us, calling us to walk in His power.

How Jesus Restores Your True Identity

Many Christians live far beneath their true calling.

The enemy deceives us into believing we are weak, sinful, and unworthy—keeping us from stepping into the fullness of our identity in Christ.

But Jesus has already settled the issue.

- **You are no longer just a sinner saved by grace**— you are a new creation (2 Corinthians 5:17).

- **You are no longer bound by fear**—you have been given a Spirit of power, love, and a sound mind (2 Timothy 1:7).

- **You are no longer separated from God**—you are one with Him in Spirit (1 Corinthians 6:17).

Jesus didn't come merely to be admired—*He came to be multiplied within us*, reproducing His life in ours.

> *I am the vine. You are the branches. He who remains in Me, and I in him, the same bears much fruit, for apart from Me you can do nothing.*
>
> *— John 15:5*

Through Him, we now carry the same Spirit that raised Christ from the dead (Romans 8:11).

Looking Ahead

We've walked with Jesus—not only as God revealed in human form, but as humanity restored to its original design: Spirit-filled, prayerful, obedient, and powerful.

He didn't just show us the Father—He showed us ourselves.

And now, He offers more than a model—He offers power.

In the next chapter, we'll discover how the same Spirit who came upon Jesus and filled Him completely now lives within us, making us God's dwelling place.

From Sinai's fire to Pentecost's flame, we'll follow the Spirit's journey—from above us to within us—transforming how we live, walk, and worship.

Reflection and Study Guide

Chapter 5: Jesus Our Model and Mediator

As He is, even so are we in this world. — 1 John 4:17

Questions for Reflection

- **Jesus as Our Example:** How does Jesus' prayer life reveal our need for daily communion with God? What simple steps can you take to align your prayer life more closely with His?

- **One Person, Fully Human:** Why is it essential to understand that Jesus was not two persons (divine and human), but one unified person? How does this deepen your trust in His ability to truly represent and redeem us?

- **Living in the Reality of Christ's Work:** Jesus said we would do *greater works* (John 14:12). What barriers—like doubt, fear, or uncertainty—keep you from fully embracing that truth?

Key Takeaways

- **Jesus Modeled a Life Filled with the Spirit:** His life didn't just reveal the Father—it showed us how to live in total dependence on the Father.

- **One Person, Not Two:** The Incarnation wasn't the union of two persons, but the full humanity of the one eternal Word becoming a true human life.

- **We Share in His Mission:** Just as Jesus received all things from the Father, He now gives us His Spirit and authority.

Practical Application

- **Follow Jesus' Prayer Pattern:** Set aside intentional time each day to pray—not just to ask, but to align your heart with the Father, just as Jesus did.

- **Step into Your Authority:** Meditate on Luke 10:19 and Ephesians 2:6. Journal how knowing you're seated with Christ changes the way you face challenges.

- **Boldly Walk in Faith:** What "greater work" is God calling you to step into this week? What practical step can you take to trust Him in that area?

Chapter 6: The Holy Spirit—God Made Tangible

The Spirit Led Israel and Now Leads You

When Jesus ascended, He didn't leave us alone—He made a way for something greater. The same Spirit who lives in Him now lives in us (Romans 8:11), leading us just as God once led Israel.

Imagine standing in the wilderness of Sinai.

The desert heat scorches your skin.

The cracked ground stretches endlessly.

The journey ahead is uncertain—until you look up.

A pillar of cloud rises into the sky.

By night, it blazes with fire, lighting the darkness.

This is no ordinary cloud. No flickering flame.

This is the presence of God.

A cloud by day to shield from the scorching sun.

A fire by night to light the path ahead.

But the wilderness was only the beginning.

The Spirit that once moved *before* them would one day move *within* us.

For generations, the Spirit moved through the Word—guiding prophets, empowering kings, and resting on chosen leaders.

Until Pentecost—when everything changed.

This was the fulfillment of Jesus' promise:

91

It is to your advantage that I go away, for if I do not go away, the Helper won't come to you. But if I go, I will send Him to you.

— *John 16:7*

Paul would later write words that would have shocked those who had only known the Spirit's power from a distance:

Do you not know that you are a temple of God, and that God's Spirit lives in you?

— *1 Corinthians 3:16*

The *fire* that once guided from without now burns *within*.

The *cloud* that once moved ahead now dwells *inside*.

For the first time, humanity carried God's presence, not just followed it.

Why the Holy Spirit Came and Went

Before Pentecost, the Spirit came and went—empowering for a moment, then departing.

But Moses longed for something more.

He had seen the Spirit's power—splitting seas, shaking mountains, speaking through fire—yet he looked ahead to a greater promise.

In Numbers 11, the Spirit came upon seventy elders, and they prophesied—but only briefly.

Then the Spirit lifted.

When Joshua objected to two men prophesying outside the gathering, Moses replied:

Are you jealous for my sake? I wish that all the LORD's people were prophets, that the LORD would put His Spirit on them!
— Numbers 11:29

This wasn't just a wish—it was a prophecy.

It shall come to pass afterward, that I will pour out My Spirit on all flesh.
— Joel 2:28

But that day had not yet come.

Until then, the Spirit moved through the Word according to God's purposes, coming upon individuals in key moments:

- **Samson** – Strengthened, then left powerless.
- **Saul** – Anointed, then tormented by spirits.
- **Elijah** – Worked miracles, then fled in despair.
- **David** – A man after God's heart, yet still pleaded:

  Do not throw me from Your presence, and do not take Your Holy Spirit from me.
  — Psalm 51:11

God's people had experienced the Spirit's power, but they lacked His abiding presence.

The Breath of Life vs. The Holy Spirit

Many assume that when God breathed life into Adam, humanity already had the Spirit, but Scripture makes a clear distinction:

- The breath of life *sustains existence.*
- The Holy Spirit *imparts divine life.*

When God formed Adam, He breathed into him, and Adam became a living soul.

But this breath was not unique to humanity—the same phrase, "breath of life," is also used for animals:

> *They* [the animals] *went to Noah into the vessel, by pairs of all flesh with the breath of life in them.*
>
> *— Genesis 7:15*

The breath of life *animated* all creatures, but it did not *transform* them.

It gave them existence, but:

- It did not make them holy.
- It did not conform them into the image of Christ.

From the very beginning, God's plan was not just to sustain us, but to *dwell within us*—to fill us with His own Spirit and transform us from the inside out.

> *A new heart also will I give you, and a new spirit will I put within you: and I will take away the stony heart out of your flesh, and I will give you a heart of flesh.*
>
> *— Ezekiel 36:26, KJV*

Something more was needed.

A Spirit that would not just animate, but *resurrect.*
A Spirit that would not just empower, but *transform.*

A Spirit that would not just return to the Father at death (Ecclesiastes 12:7), but *remain* with us forever.

> *I will dwell in them, and walk in them; and I will be their God, and they will be My people.*
> — *2 Corinthians 6:16*

But the Spirit could not come in this new way until Christ had finished His work, ascended to Heaven, and was glorified with the glory that *the Word* had before the world began.

The Holy Spirit After Jesus' Ascension

Throughout His ministry, Jesus spoke of the Holy Spirit—promising that the Spirit would guide, empower, and teach His followers.

> *He who believes in Me, as the Scripture has said, from within him will flow rivers of living water.*
> — *John 7:38*

Then comes a startling clarification:

> *He said this about the Spirit, which those believing in Him were to receive. **For the Spirit was not yet given, because Jesus was not yet glorified**.*
> — *John 7:39*

That statement should make us pause.

If the Spirit had empowered prophets and kings for generations, why does Scripture say He had not yet been given?

95

Because something greater was about to unfold.

For centuries, the Spirit came and went.

But now, through Jesus, He dwells *within* every believer, transforming us from the inside out.

The disciples didn't yet understand, but He had told them:

> *I tell you the truth: It is to your advantage that I go away, for if I do not go away, the Helper won't come to you. But if I go, I will send Him to you.*
>
> — *John 16:7*

The Spirit's full indwelling could only take place *after* Jesus' Glorification—which would allow Jesus' Spirit to be everywhere at once.

How Jesus Gives Us His Spirit

To understand how the Spirit of God now dwells within us, we must first see how the Spirit dwelt fully in Jesus.

For centuries, the eternal Word served as God's visible presence—**shielding** humanity *externally* from the fullness of the Father's transcendent glory.

But in the Incarnation, something radically new occurred: the Word didn't just take on a human body—He took on a complete human nature, including *a human spirit.*

For the first time in history, a human spirit—the sinless Spirit of Christ—became capable of receiving and containing the fullness of the Father.

Jesus likened this transformation to new wine needing a new wineskin:

> *No one puts new wine into old wineskins, or else the wine will burst the skins, and the wine is lost, and the skins will be destroyed; but one puts new wine into fresh wineskins.*
>
> *— Mark 2:22*

Before Christ, no human spirit could bear the fullness of God—we needed the Word to **shield** us *internally*.

When Jesus was glorified, something unprecedented happened: the glorified Son—fully human and fully divine—became that inner shield, the vessel that fills us with the fullness of God (Colossians 2:9–10).

> *The last Adam* [Christ] *became a life-giving Spirit.*
>
> *— 1 Corinthians 15:45*

Christ's glorified Spirit—the "new wineskin"—held the "new wine" of divine life.

And now, through spiritual union with Christ, everything in Him—the fullness of the Father—is made available to us:

> *He who is joined to the Lord is one spirit.*
>
> *— 1 Corinthians 6:17*

How the Holy Spirit Became Distinct

In the Old Testament, God's Spirit is never introduced as a distinct person speaking independently.

He is described as the breath of God—the Father's own power and presence—moving through the Word, resting upon prophets, judges, and kings.

He empowers, reveals, and acts on God's behalf, but never

speaks as an "I," nor is He addressed as a "You."

But Pentecost changed everything!

When Jesus was exalted, His human Spirit was glorified.

At that moment, the Spirit of the Father was poured into the Spirit of the Son (John 3:34)—and through the Son, poured into us.

Like the Word, the Spirit entered a new expression of distinction—not as a separate divine being, but as God's living personal presence within us.

This does not mean Jesus changed forms.

He remains forever physically enthroned in Heaven as the glorified Son of Man.

Nor does it mean the Holy Spirit began to exist at Pentecost—His activity is seen from eternity past.

But just as the Word took on personal distinction at the Incarnation by uniting with a human soul, so the Spirit took on personal distinction at Christ's glorification by uniting with a human spirit.

When Jesus was glorified, the Spirit of the Father was poured into the Spirit of the Son—uniting with and glorifying a human spirit, making it the vessel through which God's fullness could now be shared.

From this union, the Spirit begins to indwell, teach, intercede, and grieve—bearing every mark of true personal identity.

So when Jesus says, "the Spirit of your Father will speak through you" (Matthew 10:20), and Paul says, "the Spirit of Christ is in you" (Romans 8:9), they're describing the same reality: the life of the Father, flowing through the Son, now personally present within you.

> *I am in My Father… and you in Me… and I in you.*
> *— John 14:20*

Each layer forms the living bridge Jesus described:

- The Father in Christ (divine fullness).
- Christ in us, by the Spirit (glorified humanity shared).
- Us in Christ (union and identity).

In this way, the life of God flows into the hearts of men—not as three gods or mere manifestations, but as one God revealed in relational unity:

The Father as the *Source*,
The Son as the *Image*,
and the Spirit as the *Presence* within.
This is the living answer to Jesus' prayer:

> *That they may be one, just as We are one… I in them, and You in Me, that they may be perfectly one.*
> *— John 17:22–23*

Not Another Kind, but the Same Helper

Jesus did not say He would send someone entirely different. Instead, He promised to come to His disciples in a new and living way:

> *I will not leave you orphans. **I will come to you**.*
> *— John 14:18*

Just as the Son is the visible expression of the Father, the Holy Spirit is the indwelling presence of the Son—glorified, exalted, and now shared.

This is the heart of His promise:

> *I will pray to the Father, and He will give you another Helper.*
> — *John 14:16*

The Greek word for "another" is *allos*—not "another kind," but "another of the same."

This isn't someone different taking Jesus' place. It is the same Lord, now coming to dwell within us through His Spirit.

This doesn't deny the Spirit's distinction—it affirms it.

The Glorification of Christ marked the Spirit's awakening into full personhood—not as a new being, but as the very breath of the Father, now flowing through the Son's glorified humanity—alive with the heartbeat of human experience: leading, comforting, convicting, and interceding within us.

This is how Jesus fulfills His promise to come to us—by His Spirit, as the living presence of the Father and the Son.

That's why Scripture can declare:

- **2 Corinthians 3:17** – *Now the Lord is the Spirit.*
- **Colossians 1:27** – *Christ in you, the hope of glory.*
- **Galatians 4:6** – *God sent out the Spirit of His Son into our hearts, crying, "Abba, Father."*

Jesus is the One who comes to us—not in His physical form, but by His Spirit—who loves us, feels our pain, and draws us into the embrace of the Father.

He is our High Priest.
Our Life-giver.
Our indwelling Lord.

Receive the Holy Spirit

Jesus is no longer just the Word made flesh—He is now the risen and exalted Christ, *the Firstborn of a new creation.*

Before His Resurrection, Jesus lived as the perfect model of Spirit-filled humanity.

But after His Resurrection, He appeared to His disciples and did something remarkable:

> *He breathed on them, and said to them, "Receive the Holy Spirit."*
>
> *— John 20:22*

Just as God once breathed life into Adam, Jesus—now glorified—breathed on His disciples.

But this was not yet Pentecost.

Jesus had already told them to wait for something more:

> *Look, I send forth the promise of my Father on you. But wait in the city until you are clothed with power from on high.*
>
> *— Luke 24:49*

So why did He breathe on them?

Some believe this was the moment they were spiritually reborn—receiving new life through the risen Christ.

Others see it as a prophetic act—a symbolic gesture pointing ahead to Pentecost.

Perhaps it was both.

Jesus was awakening them to a deeper reality—that the breath of life, though real, was not the fullness.

They needed the Spirit—not promised, but poured out.

Not just breathed upon—but indwelling.

Not just life from Christ—but the very life of Christ within them.

What they received that day was a foretaste.

What they received at Pentecost was the fullness.

Pentecost: What Changed Forever?

Before Jesus left, He gave His disciples a final command:

> *Do not depart from Jerusalem, but wait for the promise of the Father, which you heard from Me. For John indeed baptized in water, but you will be baptized in the Holy Spirit not many days from now.*
>
> — Acts 1:4–5

Then, on Pentecost, the Spirit arrived in full power.

> *Suddenly there came from the sky a sound like the rushing of a mighty wind, and it filled all the house where they were sitting... They were all filled with the Holy Spirit.*
>
> — Acts 2:2–4

The fire that once fell on Sinai now burned *within* them.

The presence that once hid behind the veil now *filled* human hearts.

This was the moment everything had been leading to.

Pentecost was not just a new experience—*it was a new reality*.

What Moses longed for had finally come to pass.

The Spirit had come:

To indwell, not just empower.

To remain, not just visit.

To transform, not just touch.

Something greater had begun.

Looking Ahead

We've traced the Spirit's journey—from fire on the mountain to flame in the soul.

No longer hovering above, He now dwells within—God's own presence, alive in us.

But receiving the Spirit is just the beginning.

The question is:

Will we walk in His power?

In the next chapter, we'll discover how the Spirit who filled Jesus now empowers us.

We'll see how prayer unlocks authority, how obedience opens doors, and how Spirit-filled living transforms ordinary lives into vessels of the divine.

It's time to move from filled...to flowing.

Reflection and Study Guide

Chapter 6: The Holy Spirit—God Made Tangible

I will pray to the Father, and He will give you another Helper... the Spirit of truth. — John 14:16–17

Questions for Reflection

- **God's Presence in You:** In the Old Testament, the Spirit led Israel from the outside; now He dwells within us. How does His presence within you shape your identity and daily life?

- **Natural Life vs. Spiritual Life:** The breath of life made Adam a living being, but the Spirit of Christ makes us a new creation. How does this shape your understanding of salvation?

- **Walking in the Spirit:** Galatians 5:25 says, *If we live by the Spirit, let us also walk by the Spirit*. What are practical ways to stay aware of His leadings daily?

Key Takeaways

- **Jesus' Ascension Opened the Way:** The Spirit could not be fully given until Jesus was glorified, making way for His presence to dwell within us.

- **The Spirit of Christ Transforms Us:** We weren't just given new life—we were given Christ's very own Spirit, empowering us to live as sons and daughters of God.

- **The Spirit Empowers Us to Live Like Christ:** Just as Jesus walked in constant communion with the Spirit, we are called to do the same, drawing from His wisdom, power, and presence.

Practical Application

- **Invite the Spirit's Guidance Daily:** Each morning, ask the Holy Spirit to lead you. Pause throughout the day to listen for His direction.

- **Renew Your Mind to His Presence:** Meditate on Romans 8:9–11, Galatians 4:6, and Acts 1:8 to strengthen your awareness of who lives inside you.

- **Step Out in Faith:** The Spirit wasn't just given for comfort—He empowers us. Look for ways to act in His love and power—whether through prayer, sharing your faith, or using the gifts He's given you.

Chapter 7: The Holy Spirit's Power for Believers

Is It Really Possible to Live Like Jesus?

Imagine walking through the streets of Galilee.

The afternoon sun casts long shadows as dust rises beneath your feet.

You see Jesus ahead of you, moving through the crowd—not with hesitation, not with uncertainty, but with absolute confidence.

Every step is intentional.

Every word carries weight.

When He speaks, hearts burn.

When He touches, broken bodies heal.

And then He turns to you and says:

> As the Father has sent Me, even so I send you.
> — John 20:21

What if those words weren't just for the disciples—but for you? What if you weren't just meant to believe in Jesus—but also to live like Him?

At first, it sounds unthinkable.

After all, He was the Son of God.

But then, you look at the book of Acts, and you realize everything Jesus did—hearing the Father, following the Spirit, healing the sick, speaking life—the Church did, too.

Not because they had something you don't.
But because they had something you do!
The same Spirit that filled Jesus...now fills you.

The Blueprint for a Spirit-Filled Life

For centuries, people have admired Jesus.

They've studied His teachings, marveled at His miracles, and tried to imitate His kindness.

But many still assume He performed miracles simply because He was God.

Yet Scripture reveals something more profound:

- Though fully God, Jesus emptied Himself to live as a man, fully dependent on the Spirit of the Father (Philippians 2:6–7).
- He did nothing on His own—only what the Father revealed to Him (John 5:19).
- The power He walked in was the Father's Spirit working through Him (Luke 4:14).

Jesus' life wasn't just an example to admire—*it was a blueprint to follow.*

Everything He did—hearing the Father, following the Spirit, walking in power—He intended for us to do too.

That's why He told His disciples:

> *Truly, I tell you, he who believes in Me, the works that I do, he will do also; and he will do greater works than these, because I am going to the Father.*
>
> *— John 14:12*

108

Think about that.

Jesus didn't say, *The apostles will do the works I do.*
He didn't say, *Only a select few will do the works I do.*
He said, *The one who believes in Me.*

That includes you!

The disciples were filled with the same Spirit He was.
That's why their lives looked like His.
And that's why yours can too.

The Power of Jesus' Prayer Life

If you had the power to heal the sick, cast out demons, and raise the dead, what would your daily life look like?

For most people, prayer would probably take a back seat.

After all, if you can work miracles, why stop to pray?

But that's not how Jesus lived.

Even though He carried the fullness of divine power, Jesus constantly withdrew to pray.

> *Early in the morning, while it was still dark, He rose up and went out, and departed into a deserted place, and prayed there.*
>
> — *Mark 1:35*

Before every major moment, Jesus prayed.

Before choosing His disciples, He prayed all night (Luke 6:12). Before raising Lazarus, He lifted His eyes and prayed (John 11:41–42). Before facing the cross, He agonized in prayer (Luke 22:41–44).

Prayer wasn't just something Jesus *did*—it was the source of His strength.

Every miracle flowed from His communion with the Father. And if Jesus *needed* prayer, how much more do we?

The Early Church understood this.

Before Pentecost, they prayed for the Spirit (Acts 1:14).

After persecution, they prayed for boldness (Acts 4:29–31).

When Peter was imprisoned, they prayed and an angel set him free (Acts 12:5–7).

Prayer wasn't a religious duty—it was their lifeline to supernatural power.

To walk in the Spirit, *we must live a life of prayer*.

Why Prayer Feels Hard (How to Fix It)

Many Christians struggle with prayer.

They try to talk to God—but often feel like He's silent.

Why does prayer feel so difficult?

Because deep down, many believe a lie:

- God doesn't speak to people like me.

- I'm not spiritual enough to hear His voice.

- What if it's just my own thoughts?

These doubts are some of the enemy's most effective weapons. Because if we doubt God's voice, we'll always second guess His leading.

But here's the truth—God wants to speak to you.

That's why He gave you His Spirit—to help you hear Him.

The more you step into prayer, the clearer His voice becomes.

> *My sheep hear My voice, and I know them, and they follow Me.*
> — *John 10:27*

Hearing God isn't just for pastors or "special Christians." It's for every believer—*including you.*

How to Follow Jesus' Example in Prayer

- **Believe that God will speak**—and that you can hear Him.
- **Make time for prayer**—not as a ritual, but as your lifeline.
- **Learn to listen**—prayer isn't just talking; it's also receiving.

How Jesus Was Led by the Holy Spirit

Imagine standing at the Pool of Bethesda.

The air is thick with suffering.

Dozens of sick, paralyzed, and blind people lie on mats—waiting, hoping—for a miracle.

Then Jesus steps in.

What would you expect?

Would He walk through the crowd, healing everyone?

Instead, He does something surprising.

He passes by many, approaches one crippled man, and asks:

> *Do you want to be made well?*
> *— John 5:6*

The man nods. With a single command, Jesus heals him.
But why only him?
Why not heal everyone?
Later, Jesus gives the answer:

> *The Son can do nothing of Himself, but what He sees the Father doing.*
> *— John 5:19*

Jesus wasn't led by need alone.
He wasn't led by human expectation.
He was led by the Spirit of God.
Every step He took, every word He spoke, every miracle He performed—it was all directed by the Father:

> *For I spoke not from Myself, but the Father who sent Me, He gave Me a commandment, what I should say, and what I should speak.*
> *— John 12:49*

This is why His life was so powerful.
This is why His ministry was so effective.
Jesus wasn't just doing *good* things—He was doing *God's* things.
And this is where it gets exciting...

The Spirit Moved—And Still Does Today

The Spirit didn't just lead Jesus—He continued to move through His followers in Acts.

And He still moves today.

> *As they served the Lord and fasted, the Holy Spirit said, "Separate Barnabas and Saul for Me, for the work to which I have called them."*
>
> *— Acts 13:2*

The Early Church didn't just make strategic plans.
They didn't rely on logic or leadership models.
They listened for the Spirit's direction.
And because they did, miracles followed.

Philip and the Ethiopian Official (Acts 8:29–35)

Philip wasn't an apostle.
He wasn't a Church leader.
He was simply a man willing to listen.
While traveling one day, the Spirit spoke:

> *The Spirit said to Philip, "Go and join up with that chariot."*
>
> *— Acts 8:29*

Philip obeyed.

Inside the chariot, an Ethiopian official was reading Isaiah. Philip explained the Gospel, and by the end of the conversation, the man believed and was baptized.

One prompting from the Spirit changed a life forever.

Peter and the Beggar at the Temple (Acts 3:1–10)

One afternoon, Peter and John were walking into the temple when a beggar asked them for money.

Peter could have ignored him.

But the Spirit stirred something inside.

Instead of handing over coins, Peter locked eyes with the man and said:

> *Silver and gold have I none, but what I have, that I give you. In the name of Jesus Christ the Nazorean, get up and walk.*
>
> *— Acts 3:6*

In an instant, the man was healed.

Jesus had healed by the Spirit.

Now His followers were doing the same.

Paul's Missionary Journey (Acts 16:6–10)

Paul had a plan.

He intended to preach the Gospel in Asia.

It was logical.

It was strategic.

It was good.

But the Spirit stopped him.

> *They were forbidden by the Holy Spirit to speak the Word in Asia.*
>
> — *Acts 16:6*

That night, Paul had a vision of a man from Macedonia saying, "Come help us."

So Paul changed course.

Because he obeyed, the Gospel spread to an entire region—Philippi, Thessalonica, Corinth, and beyond.

Paul's logic said "Go to Asia."

The Spirit said "Go to Macedonia."

And because he followed, Europe was never the same.

The Spirit Is Personal—Not Just Power

The Holy Spirit doesn't just move through us—He walks with us. He doesn't just empower moments—He builds relationship.

Many believers think of the Holy Spirit as a force—an invisible power source we tap into when we need help.

But Scripture reveals something far more personal:

- **The Spirit speaks**: *Separate Barnabas and Saul... for the work to which I have called them* (Acts 13:2).

- **The Spirit teaches**: *He will teach you all things* (John 14:26).

- **The Spirit grieves**: *Do not grieve the Holy Spirit* (Ephesians 4:30).

This isn't just divine energy.

This is God Himself—living and active, guiding us moment by moment.

He's not just fire—He is the Spirit of Christ.

Our Comforter.

Our Guide.

Our Friend.

Why Hearing the Holy Spirit Feels Hard

Most Christians don't struggle to hear God—they struggle to trust that it's really Him speaking.

We overthink.

We hesitate.

We second-guess what we sense.

So instead of listening to the Spirit, we lean on our own logic.

But the Spirit rarely reveals the full plan.

He gives one step—then waits for obedience.

Your word is a lamp to my feet, and a light for my path.
— Psalm 119:105

A lamp doesn't show the whole road.

It shows the next step.

Even Jesus experienced this.

As the Son of Man, He didn't always walk in full understanding:

*But no one knows of that day and hour, not even the angels of Heaven, **nor the Son**, but My Father only.*
— *Matthew 24:36*

If Jesus—God in the flesh—had to trust the Father completely, how much more must we?

Trust wasn't optional for Jesus. It isn't for us either.

How to Walk in the Spirit Like Jesus

- **Ask** the Spirit for direction—then *expect* an answer.
- **Act** on what you hear—even if it's just *one* small step.
- **Trust** God to guide you—even when the full picture isn't clear.

Most people wait for clarity before they obey.
But clarity comes through obedience.

If we live by the Spirit, let us also walk by the Spirit.
— *Galatians 5:25*

Discerning the Spirit's Voice

Not every prompting comes from the Holy Spirit.
But God gives us ways to recognize His voice.

1. **The Scripture Test:** *Does it align with the Bible?*

The Spirit never contradicts the Word—He inspired it (2 Timothy 3:16).

2. **The Fruit Test:** *Does it bear the character of Christ?*

Love. Joy. Peace. Patience. Kindness. Humility.
The flesh pushes, but the Spirit gently draws.

3. The Peace Test: *Does it bring deep, spiritual clarity?*

God is not the author of confusion (1 Corinthians 14:33).
Peace is not just comfort—but also quiet confidence.

Still unsure? Pause. Pray. Get wise counsel.
The Holy Spirit is not in a hurry—*He's after relationship,* not performance.

How the Trinity Flows Through You

In the opening words of Acts, Luke gives us a subtle but powerful insight:

> *The first account I wrote, Theophilus, concerned all that Jesus **began** both to do and to teach.*
> — *Acts 1:1*

Did you catch that?
Began.
Luke didn't say, *all that Jesus did and taught.*
He said, *all that Jesus began to do and teach.*
Jesus' earthly ministry wasn't the end—it was the beginning.
His work of atonement was finished, but His mission was just getting started.
And He never intended to do it alone (Matthew 28:18–20).

As the Father has sent Me, even so I send you.
— John 20:21

Jesus came to reveal the Father, walk in the Spirit, and bring the Kingdom.

Now, through the Spirit, He continues that work—through us.

How Jesus Multiplies His Power Through You

During His earthly ministry, Jesus was limited to one place at one time.

If He was in Galilee, He wasn't in Jerusalem.

If He was in a boat, He wasn't in the temple.

But through the Spirit, He multiplies His presence in us.

His presence is no longer confined to one place—it's wherever you and I go.

Your Calling: Bringing Heaven to Earth

All things are of God, who reconciled us to Himself through Jesus Christ, and gave to us the ministry of reconciliation.
— 2 Corinthians 5:18

Jesus came to restore the world—and now, we carry on His mission.

- Just as He revealed the Father, so do we.
- Just as He moved in the Spirit, so do we.
- Just as He walked in love and power, so do we.

We don't just represent Him—we continue His work.
Like Jesus, this is the pattern we are meant to walk in:

FATHER —> SON (His Body) —> SPIRIT —> WORLD

The pattern hasn't changed.
But now, *you're a part of it*!
Stop waiting for permission—or the perfect moment.

Pray. Listen. Obey. Love.
And watch the Spirit move.
Step out. Take your place. The world is waiting.

Looking Ahead

We've seen what's possible when believers walk in the Spirit—when prayer becomes power, and obedience opens doors.

Jesus didn't just model that life—He multiplied it through His Church.

But what happened to that power?

In the next chapter, we'll uncover how the Early Church was filled with miracles—and how, over time, theology replaced experience.

We'll trace the shift from fire to form and rediscover the divine pattern that was never meant to fade.

It's time to confront what was lost—and reclaim what still burns.

Reflection and Study Guide

Chapter 7: The Holy Spirit's Power for Believers

You will receive power when the Holy Spirit has come upon you. You will be My witnesses. — Acts 1:8

Questions for Reflection

- **The Spirit's Power in You:** How does knowing that the same Spirit who empowered Jesus now dwells in you reshape how you view your daily life?

- **Hearing and Trusting the Spirit:** Jesus was led by the Spirit in everything. How do you recognize when the Spirit is leading you? What holds you back from fully trusting His guidance?

- **Stepping Out in Faith:** The Spirit rarely reveals the full picture—He leads one step at a time. Is there an area in your life where God is prompting you to take a step of faith, even if you don't yet see the whole path?

Key Takeaways

- **The Spirit Empowers Every Believer:** The same Spirit who filled Jesus now fills you, equipping you to walk in His love, wisdom, and power.

- **Obedience Unlocks More of the Spirit's Leading:** The Spirit often speaks through small promptings. As you step out in faith, His direction and power become clearer.

- **The Spirit's Work is Ongoing:** Jesus' earthly ministry was just the beginning. Through the Spirit, His mission continues in and through His people today.

Practical Application

- **Start Your Day with the Spirit:** Before doing anything else, invite the Holy Spirit to guide your thoughts, words, and actions. Ask Him to lead you in ways that reflect Jesus.

- **Act on a Prompting:** When you sense the Spirit nudging you—whether to pray for someone, speak encouragement, or take a bold step—respond immediately and trust the outcome to God.

- **Stay in Step with the Spirit:** Read Acts 1–2 and reflect on how the Early Church depended on the Spirit. Ask God to renew that same dependence in your life.

PART 3—EXPERIENCING GOD

Living in the Trinity's Power

Chapter 8: When Theology Replaced Experience

When Miracles Were Normal

The river roared, swallowing fields, homes, and roads.

Its waters surged down from the mountains, tearing through the land with unstoppable fury.

Banks collapsed.

Trees were ripped from their roots.

Entire villages faced destruction.

Panic spread.

No dam could hold it back.

No human effort could stand against its wrath.

With nowhere left to turn, the people sought the only man they believed could help—not a ruler, not an engineer, but a bishop known for his unshakable faith.

He came with no armies.

No tools.

Only his staff and his prayers.

Walking to the river's edge, he lifted his hands to heaven and called upon God's power. Then, kneeling on the saturated ground, he drove his staff into the earth.

From that day forward, no matter how fiercely the river swelled, the water halted at the very place he had marked.

In time, a tree grew in the place his staff had been—becoming a living boundary that stood against the flood for generations to come.

For years, people watched in awe as the surging waters never passed the tree's roots. The river bent around the spot in reverence, as if restrained by an unseen force.

This was not a story from the Book of Acts.

Nor was it a legend from ancient Israel.

It happened in the third century.

Long after the apostles died, the power of God remained.

The man's name was Gregory Thaumaturgus—Gregory the Wonderworker, and the city was Neocaesarea.

When he arrived, only seventeen believers lived there.

By the time he died, only seventeen unbelievers remained.

This event was recorded by Gregory of Nyssa (335–395 AD), a respected Church theologian, in his work *Life of Gregory Thaumaturgus*, where he recounts the many miracles God performed through him.

In Neocaesarea, the sick were healed, demons were cast out, and the dead were raised to life.

Gregory even foresaw future events before they happened.

This city knew that the acts of the apostles had not ended.

The Spirit of God had not faded.

The miracles had not ceased.

Eyewitnesses of the Miraculous

These weren't isolated stories. Respected leaders in the Early Church testified that miracles were still happening.

Justin Martyr (100–165 AD), a bold Christian writer who defended the faith against Roman persecution, spoke of believers casting out demons and healing in the name of Jesus—something he said was happening all over the world:

For numberless demoniacs throughout the whole world, and in your city, many of our Christian men exorcising them in the name of Jesus Christ... have healed and do heal, rendering helpless and driving the possessing devils out of the men.

— Justin Martyr, *Second Apology*, Chapter 6

Irenaeus (130–202 AD), a disciple of Polycarp (who was a direct disciple of the Apostle John), affirmed that miracles were still happening in his day:

Those who are in truth His disciples, receiving grace from Him, do in His name perform [miracles], so as to promote the welfare of other men... the dead even have been raised up, and remained among us.

— Irenaeus, *Against Heresies*, Book 2, Chapter 32

Origen (185–254 AD), a teacher and writer who boldly defended Christianity against philosophers who mocked miracles, declared:

There are still preserved among Christians traces of that Holy Spirit which appeared in the form of a dove. They expel evil spirits, and perform many cures, and foresee certain events, according to the will of the Logos.

— Origen, *Against Celsus*, Book 1, Chapter 46

To the Early Church, moving in God's power was normal. And why wouldn't it be?

To them, Jesus' words were not mere history—they were a present reality:

Truly, I tell you, he who believes in Me, the works that I do, he will do also.

— John 14:12

For three centuries, believers did not separate themselves from the story of Acts. The same Spirit who empowered Jesus had been poured out upon them.

They weren't just studying the Trinity—*they were living it.*

Basil the Great (330–379 AD), a powerful preacher who defended the Holy Spirit's role in the life of believers, emphasized the transformative work of the Holy Spirit:

> *Through the Holy Spirit comes our restoration to paradise, our ascension into the Kingdom of Heaven, our return to the adoption of sons, our liberty to call God our Father, our being made partakers of the grace of Christ.*
>
> — Basil the Great, *On the Holy Spirit*, Chapter 15

The Early Church had a clear vision of how the Trinity worked as one.

They saw God's divine pattern at work:

Father —> Son (through His Body) —> Spirit —> World

The Father was still speaking.
The Son was still moving through His people.
The Spirit was still breathing life into the world.

Why Miracles Began to Fade

For centuries, the Church moved in undeniable power.

Healings, prophecy, and deliverance were not rare occurrences—they were the norm.

Then, a turning point came that altered the course of Church history.

By the end of the fourth century, miracles—once common —had become rare. Not because God withdrew His power, but because the Church drifted from it.

Two major events seem to have contributed to this decline:

- **380 AD:** *Theodosius I issued the Edict of Thessalonica,* making Nicene Christianity the official state religion of the Roman Empire.

- **381 AD:** *The Council of Constantinople finalized the doctrine of the Trinity*—unintentionally transforming it from a lived reality to a studied belief.

Just forty years later, in 420 AD, Augustine of Hippo—one of the most influential voices in the post-Constantinian Church —acknowledged the disappearance of miracles:

> *Why, they say, are those miracles, which you affirm were wrought formerly, wrought no longer? I might, indeed, reply that miracles were necessary before the world believed, in order that it might believe.*
>
> — Augustine, *The City of God*, Book 22, Chapter 8

As the Church's influence in society grew, its relational view of the Trinity began to drift. What had once been a movement fueled by divine power became a structured institution.

Slowly but surely, the Church transitioned from *experiencing* God to merely *explaining* Him.

The Trinity: A Puzzle or a Pattern?

To the earliest Christians, the Trinity was not an abstract doctrine—it was the heartbeat of their faith.

Gregory of Nyssa (335–395 AD) described how God moves in the world, revealing the Trinity's divine pattern:

> *Every operation which extends from God to the Creation, and is named according to our variable conceptions of it, has its origin from the Father, and proceeds through the Son, and is perfected in the Holy Spirit.*
>
> — Gregory of Nyssa, *On "Not Three Gods"*

Irenaeus described the work of the Trinity as the *two hands of the Father*—working together.

> *Now man... was formed after the likeness of God, and moulded by His hands, that is, by the Son and Holy Spirit.*
>
> — Irenaeus, *Against Heresies,* Book 4, Preface

When the Church cooperated in harmony with this divine pattern, they saw the same results as Jesus.

The Power Was Never Meant to Stop

This shift—from relationship to ritual—was neither sudden nor imposed.

It crept in so subtly that few realized what was being lost.

But not everyone believed that miracles had ceased.

Even Augustine, who once questioned their absence, would later reverse his stance.

He documented numerous healings, exorcisms, and even resurrections—many of which he personally witnessed.

> *Even now, therefore, many miracles are wrought, the same God who wrought those we read of still performing them, by whom He will and as He will.*
> — Augustine, *The City of God*, Book 22, Chapter 8

Across his writings, Augustine attested to dozens of miracles—some scholars estimate more than seventy.

Just a few of the miracles he recorded include:

- A man in Milan was instantly healed of blindness.
- A terminally ill woman in Carthage was cured of breast cancer.
- A man paralyzed by gout was healed at baptism.
- A man violently tormented by demons was set free.
- A priest named Eucharius, declared dead, was restored to life.
- A poor Christian tailor, in desperate need, prayed—and found gold in a fish's belly.

  (All from *The City of God*, Book 22, Chapter 8)

These were not ancient legends or distant memories.

They were firsthand accounts—documented by one of the most respected theologians in Church history.

Miracles were still happening.
God had not changed.

Doctrine Without Relationship

Jesus warned against trying to find life in the Scriptures alone:

> *You search the Scriptures, because you think that in them you have everlasting life; and these are they which testify about Me. But you are unwilling to come to Me so that you may have life.*
>
> *— John 5:39–40*

The Bible points us to Jesus, but it's our *relationship with Him*—living in the reality of the Trinity—that brings life.

The Early Church faced a choice:

Would they continue participating in God's power, or reduce Him to a doctrine to debate?

Today, we face the same choice.

The miracles of the Early Church are not relics of history— they are the natural result of believers partnering with the Trinity's divine pattern.

The question is not whether the Spirit is still moving.

The question is:

Are we listening to the Father's voice, obeying like the Son, and walking the Holy Spirit's power?

Restoring the Gospel of Power

The book of Acts was never meant to be a record of the past. It was always meant to be a blueprint for the present.

132

Jesus Christ is the same yesterday, today, and forever.
— Hebrews 13:8

The world doesn't need more institutions. It needs burning ones—people ablaze with the fire of God.

It needs people who don't just study God's power but walk in it, release it, and transform lives.

You're called to more than belief. You're called to action.

Will you commune in prayer, hear God's voice, and obey?

The Spirit never stopped moving.

The only question is—*will you?*

Looking Ahead

The Early Church didn't just believe—they walked with God. But when theology replaced experience, the Gospel was reduced to a theory, and the Trinity became a puzzle.

What was once a fire became a form.

Yet the Spirit never left.

In the next chapter, we'll uncover how distortions of the Trinity—like Tritheism, Modalism, and Arianism—fractured the Gospel itself.

We'll trace how the united God of Scripture was divided by doctrine—and how salvation was reshaped into something He never intended.

But we won't stop there.

We'll recover the original vision—where Father, Son, and Spirit move in perfect unity to restore all things.

It's time to confront the fractures—and reclaim the Gospel's full power.

Reflection and Study Guide

Chapter 8: When Theology Replaced Experience

Contend earnestly for the faith which was once for all delivered to the saints. — Jude 1:3

Questions for Reflection

- **Experiencing vs. Explaining God:** The Early Church didn't just study the Trinity—they lived in its power. Are there areas in your life where you're explaining God more than experiencing Him?

- **The Shift from Power to Institution:** What key moments led to the decline of miracles in the Church? How can we avoid prioritizing structure over the Spirit —in our churches and in our personal lives?

- **Walking in the Divine Pattern:** The Father's will is revealed through the Son and carried out by the Spirit. What steps can you take to live in this reality?

Key Takeaways

- **The Early Church Moved in Power:** For the first three centuries, believers didn't separate themselves from the book of Acts. The same Spirit who empowered Jesus and the apostles continued working through them.

- **Faith Shifted from Encounter to Concept:** As the Church became more structured, defining God often replaced experiencing Him. The Trinity shifted from a lived reality to a theological discussion.

- **The Power Was Never Meant to Stop:** The Trinity still empowers the Church today. The Spirit hasn't stopped moving—we must choose to walk according to God's divine pattern.

Practical Application

- **Pursue Presence Over Theory:** Set aside intentional time this week to seek the Holy Spirit's presence. Ask Him to reveal Himself in ways that go beyond theology and into encounter.

- **Break Out of Routine:** Identify one area in your life or church where tradition has replaced transformation. Ask God for fresh hunger—and renewed expectation of His power.

- **Take a Step of Faith:** Act on what the Spirit is stirring in you. Whether it's praying for healing, sharing the Gospel, or obeying a quiet prompting— trust that God still moves through those who listen and respond.

Chapter 9: Fracturing the Gospel and Godhead

The Gospel of Power in the Early Church

Jerusalem stirred with unrest.

A miracle had shaken the temple courts—a man born lame now stood upright, walking and leaping in praise.

Peter, filled with the Holy Spirit, declared without fear:

> By the name of Jesus Christ of Nazareth, whom you crucified, whom God raised from the dead—by Him this man is standing before you well.
>
> — Acts 4:10, ESV

The authorities were enraged.

But the people were in awe.

Something had shifted.

Heaven was breaking into earth.

> There is salvation in none other, for there is no other name under Heaven... by which we must be saved.
>
> — Acts 4:12

This was not a message of survival or escape—but the arrival of a victorious Kingdom.

Christ had conquered.

The Spirit had come.

The Father's plan had prevailed.

137

A Gospel Divided Is a Godhead Distorted

Peter walked in power because he understood the real story of salvation (Acts 2:23–24; 3:14–15; 4:10).

He knew this wasn't a story of a divided Trinity—a *wrathful* Father demanding punishment from His innocent Son.

It was humanity's violence—met not with wrath, but with mercy, healing, and the resurrection power of a *loving* Father.

Men had crucified Jesus.

But God had raised Him from the dead.

And now, everything had changed:

- Christ broke the power of sin.
- He conquered death.
- He overthrew the dominion of Satan.

His Resurrection wasn't just a personal triumph—it was the Father's victory, unleashing a new creation into the earth.

This was the Gospel that shook the ancient world.

The Unified Work of the Trinity

From the beginning, the Gospel was never about a divided God seeking retribution.

It was the outworking of one God—united in essence, undivided in will—moving in love to bring restoration.

The early Christians understood salvation as the harmonious work of the Father, Son, and Spirit:

- No tension between justice and love.
- No division between the Father's will and the Son's mission.

- No absence of the Spirit's presence and power.

They saw every act of redemption as the unified flow of the Trinity—moving together in relational harmony.

> *The Father is indeed above all, and He is the Head of Christ; but the Word is through all things, and is Himself the Head of the Church; while the Spirit is in us all, and He is the living water, which the Lord grants to those who rightly believe in Him, and love Him.*
> — Irenaeus, *Against Heresies*, Book 5, Chapter 18

- **The Father *initiates* salvation**—sending the Son in love to reconcile the world to Himself (John 3:16).
- **The Son *accomplishes* salvation**—taking on human nature to defeat sin and death (Hebrews 2:14).
- **The Spirit *applies* salvation**—transforming us into the likeness of Christ (2 Corinthians 3:18).

But over time, the Church began to drift.

As confusion about the Trinity's oneness deepened, even the meaning of the cross began to shift.

The Gospel became a legal transaction between two parties —casting the Father as distant, detached, and wrathful.

How Atonement Became Divided

For the first three centuries, the Gospel was proclaimed as divine victory—Father, Son, and Spirit moving together as one in perfect love to redeem and restore humanity.

But as distortions of the Trinity took root, atonement itself was reshaped.

Any view of atonement that divides God inevitably distorts salvation.

Let's examine three historic distortions—Tritheism, Modalism, and Arianism—and how each reshaped the Gospel into something it was never meant to be.

Tritheism: A Divided God, A Divided Gospel

Tritheism imagines the Father, Son, and Spirit as three separate beings—fracturing God's unity and undermining His nature as one.

This fractured view of God laid the groundwork for atonement theories that pitted the Father and the Son against each other—especially:

- *Satisfaction Theory* (11th century, Anselm)
- *Penal Substitution Theory* (16th century, Protestant Reformers)

Though Anselm and the Reformers affirmed the Trinity, their models portrayed a God divided against Himself—one person demanding punishment, another pleading for mercy.

But Jesus said He only does what He sees the Father doing.

> *Truly, I tell you, the Son can do nothing of Himself, but what He sees the Father doing. For whatever things He does, these the Son also does likewise.*
>
> *— John 5:19*

If wrath were the Father's will, Jesus would have mirrored it. Instead, Jesus forgave freely (John 8:1–11, Luke 23:34).

Penal Substitution misrepresents the Trinity.

It portrays a *transactional* God: a Father appeased by the suffering of an innocent Son.

But this isn't how love works.

And it's not how God's justice works, either.

> The soul who sins, he shall die: the son shall not bear the iniquity of the father... the righteousness of the righteous shall be on him, and the wickedness of the wicked shall be on him.
>
> — Ezekiel 18:20

God does not punish one person to forgive another.

Even when Moses offered to be punished in Israel's place, God refused (Exodus 32:32–33).

Yet this same logic gets read into the Old Testament sacrifices, but Scripture is clear that the sacrifices were about cleansing, not punishment:

> The blood of goats and bulls... sanctify to the **cleanness** of the flesh: how much more will the blood of Christ... **cleanse** our conscience from dead works to serve the living God?
>
> — Hebrews 9:13–14

The scapegoat—the only animal that symbolically bore sin in the Old Covenant—was *released*, not killed (Leviticus 16:21–22). This one detail dismantles the very foundation of Penal Substitution's reading of the sacrificial system.

Jesus didn't hang on the cross to satisfy divine wrath.

He died to:

- Fulfill the Old Covenant's exit clause—the curse of the Law (Deuteronomy 28; Galatians 3:13–14).

- Abolish the legal system that condemned even the innocent (Colossians 2:14).

- Establish a New Covenant—to cleanse and restore us to God (Luke 22:20; Hebrews 9:14).

- Break the power of sin (Romans 6:6–7), death (Romans 8:2), and the devil (Hebrews 2:14).

But What About Propitiation?

*Whom God hath set forth to be a **propitiation** [hilastérion] through faith in his blood.*

— Romans 3:25 (KJV)

In pagan culture, *hilastērion* referred to appeasing the wrath of the gods.

But in Jewish thought—as seen in the Septuagint and in Hebrews 9:5—it referred to something entirely different:

*The cherubims of glory shadowing the **mercyseat** [hilastérion].*

— Hebrews 9:5 (KJV)

Jesus is not the object of wrath—He is the place of mercy, the living Mercy Seat where union with God is restored.

The Cross is not where God poured out His anger.

It is where God poured out His heart.

Modalism: A Hollow Gospel Without the Trinity

Modalism teaches that God is one Person who merely plays different roles—appearing sometimes as Father, sometimes as Son, and sometimes as Spirit.

But this collapses God's nature into a performance—like an actor switching roles on a stage—and undermines the love shared between the Father, Son, and Spirit.

Without personal distinction, there can be no sending, no receiving, and no true self-giving love—only divine monologue disguised as dialogue.

This is the root flaw behind *Governmental Theory* (16th century, Hugo Grotius), which portrays God as a moral governor who must uphold justice by making an example of sin.

In this view, Jesus doesn't bear our sin—He simply suffers, like an actor, to demonstrate how serious sin is.

At first glance, it may sound more merciful than Penal Substitution—it doesn't portray the Father punishing the Son.

Yet it still fractures the Gospel: God's "solution" to sin becomes a public demonstration—a theatrical show—not a personal rescue.

But Scripture completely contradicts this idea:

> *We speak God's wisdom in a mystery... which none of the rulers of this age has understood. For had they known it, they would not have crucified the Lord of glory.*
>
> — *1 Corinthians 2:7–8*

If the cross were meant to publicly display divine justice, then it failed—because the world didn't even recognize what God was doing.

The cross was not a spectacle for human judgment.

It was a hidden rescue, revealed only by the Spirit.

Yet in Governmental Theory, the Spirit is functionally absent. The cross becomes a legal backdrop for forgiveness—not a living doorway into transformation.

But Scripture doesn't say Christ died to make a statement. It says:

- He came to destroy the works of the devil (1 John 3:8).
- He came to cleanse our conscience (Hebrews 9:14).
- He came to pour out the Spirit into our hearts (Galatians 4:6).

Governmental Theory may preserve God's image as Judge, but—like Modalism—it loses His heart as Father.

The result?

A distant, impersonal, powerless salvation—*a hollow gospel* that enforces God's law but never restores God's love.

Arianism: A Lesser Christ, A Weaker Gospel

Arianism denied Christ's full divinity, reducing Him to a created being—greater than man, but less than God.

But if Jesus is not fully God, then salvation collapses before it begins. No created being can overcome sin, conquer death, or unite us with divine life.

Only God can save—and only a fully divine Christ could restore what was broken.

That's why Scripture says: *He* [Jesus] *is the radiance of His* [the Father's] *glory, the very image of His substance* (Hebrews 1:3), and *it pleased the Father that in Him* [Christ] *should all fulness dwell* (Colossians 1:19, KJV).

Arianism didn't just distort Christ—it replaced divine power with moral effort, victory with inspiration, and atonement with nothing more than an example.

This laid the foundation for *Moral Influence Theory* (12th century, Peter Abelard), which taught that Jesus died not to destroy sin but to move us emotionally—showing us how far love will go.

In this view, the cross becomes a symbol to awaken repentance, not a battle to defeat evil.

Salvation shifts from rescue to response.

Abelard considered himself Trinitarian, but like Arianism, his theology denied the necessity of a divine Redeemer—reducing Christ to a moral example, not a conquering King; and atonement to motivation, not transformation.

But we don't need a martyr to inspire us.

We need a Messiah to deliver us.

> *The blood of Jesus, His Son, cleanses us from all sin.*
> — *1 John 1:7*

God didn't give us a symbol. He gave us a Savior—a Son, radiant in glory, full of divinity, and crowned with victory.

Why This Still Matters Today

Each of these theologians *claimed* to be Trinitarian—yet each drifted into a distorted view of God and the Gospel:

- **Tritheism** produced a *divided atonement* — where the Father demands and the Son absorbs (Satisfaction / Penal Substitution).

- **Modalism** produced a *legalistic atonement* — where justice is upheld through theater, not transformation (Governmental Theory).

- **Arianism** produced a *powerless atonement* — where Christ merely inspires but did not conquer (Moral Influence Theory).

The Early Church fiercely rejected any theology that weakened Christ's divinity or fractured the Trinity's unity in salvation.

Salvation isn't the story of a divided God.

It is the story of one God—Father, Son, and Spirit—moving in perfect unity to rescue, redeem, and restore.

The Gospel is not about us working our way back to God.

It is about the Father sending the Son in the power of the Spirit to bring Heaven to earth.

And as this chapter has shown:

The Trinity is not just a doctrine to affirm—it is a lens to discern.

When theology divides the Trinity, it distorts the Gospel and must be rejected as error.

But when we return to the unity of Father, Son, and Spirit, we recover a Gospel of love, power, and transformation—one that opens our eyes to the truth.

The Atonement Views of the Early Church

By the second century, the Church upheld two primary atonement views—both rooted in the teachings of the apostles.

These early models weren't abandoned for lack of clarity, but were later overshadowed by frameworks shaped by law, fear, and Greek speculation.

- **Recapitulation (2nd century, Irenaeus)**

  Christ, the Second Adam, retraced humanity's journey and redeemed it by succeeding where Adam failed. Through His Incarnation, obedience, death, and Resurrection, He restored our nature, reunited us with God, and secured our transformation into His likeness.

- **Christus Victor (2nd century, Irenaeus)**

  Through His death and Resurrection, Christ triumphed over sin, conquered death, and overthrew the devil— liberating humanity from bondage and restoring God's reign over creation.

These are the *only* atonement views with a clear historical lineage from the disciples of the apostles—especially Irenaeus, who was taught by Polycarp, a disciple of John.

Each view upheld:

- A unified Trinity.
- A fully divine Christ
- A salvation that was not transactional, but transformative.

These views resisted Greek metaphysics and gave the Church a Gospel both cosmic in scope and personal in power.

It wasn't until the third century that a new theory—*Ransom to Satan*—emerged, subtly shifting the focus from Christ's victory to a cosmic negotiation.

From there, atonement theology began to fracture.

Why does this matter?

Because our atonement theology shapes our view of God.

If we lose sight of the Early Church's vision, we risk distorting—not just the Trinity—but the Gospel itself.

Whenever atonement divides God, it distorts salvation.

The Father, Son, and Spirit are not in conflict.

They are not distant from one another.

They are not competing forces in redemption.

Salvation is the Trinity at work in perfect harmony.

Returning to the Divine Pattern

History reveals a painful shift: the Church lost sight of the Trinity's unity—and with it, the lens through which Scripture was meant to be read.

But we are not bound by history.

The Spirit is still moving.
The Trinity is still restoring.
The victory of Christ is still advancing.
The only question is: *Will we return?*

Will we recover the divine pattern of the Early Church?

Will we proclaim a God who is truly one—Father, Son, and Spirit—moving in perfect harmony to redeem all things?

This isn't just a call to better theology.

It's a call to reclaim the Gospel of the Kingdom—to live as those who believe: *Christ has conquered.*

The Spirit is with us.
The Kingdom is advancing.
And nothing will stand against it.
The time for explanation is over.
It's time to live in the reality of God.

Looking Ahead

This chapter revealed how Tritheism, Modalism, and Arianism fractured not just doctrine—but the Gospel.

But what if those same distortions also shape how we read Scripture?

In the next chapter, we return to the beginning—revisiting stories that have long stirred fear, confusion, or doubt.

From Eden to Amalek, from Noah's flood to Sodom's fall, we'll see how Christ reframes them all.

Because once the veil is lifted:

Justice looks different.
Wrath finds its purpose.
And God's heart comes into focus.

The Gospel is not a courtroom drama.

It is the Father, Son, and Spirit stepping into our world, conquering sin, and embracing us in divine love.

Reflection and Study Guide

Chapter 9: Fracturing the Gospel and Godhead

For in Him all the fullness of God was pleased to dwell, and through Him to reconcile to Himself all things. — Colossians 1:19–20, ESV

Questions for Reflection

- **Tritheism and Atonement:** How does viewing the atonement as the unified work of the Trinity confront the idea of a divided God?

- **Arianism and Atonement:** Why is Christ's full divinity essential for reconciling creation to the Father?

- **Harmony of the Trinity:** How does understanding the atonement as the unified work of the Father, Son, and Spirit deepen your worship and gratitude?

Key Takeaways

- **Unity in the Atonement**: The Father, Son, and Spirit work inseparably in creation, redemption, and glorification.

- **Contrast with Errors**: Tritheism fractures God's unity, Modalism flattens His relational nature, and Arianism denies Christ's divinity—each distorting the atonement's true nature.

- **Trinitarian Harmony**: The biblical atonement reveals the triune God's justice, love, and mercy as one seamless, restorative act.

Practical Application

- **Meditate on Unity**: Spend time this week reflecting on the relational harmony of the Trinity in salvation. How does this shape your worship and prayer life?

- **Recognize Errors**: Identify any misconceptions about the atonement you've held or encountered. How can the relational unity of the Trinity correct these views?

- **Celebrate the Trinity in Worship**: Whether in personal devotion or corporate worship, acknowledge how each Person of the Trinity moves in your salvation. Let this awareness deepen your gratitude and praise.

Chapter 10: Christ—The True Lens to See God

A New Way to See God

One question has echoed through the centuries:

Is the God of the Old Testament the same as Jesus?

At first glance, the contrast seems undeniable—a wrathful Old Testament Judge and a merciful New Testament Savior.

Even in Jesus' day, many saw God as eager to punish His enemies and enforce rigid legalism.

But when Jesus came, He shattered their expectations.

He revealed something far greater:

- A Father longing to restore rather than condemn.

- A God whose justice is inseparable from mercy.

- A King who conquers not by violence but by sacrificial love.

Jesus didn't come to change God's nature—*He came to reveal it.*

Many Old Testament passages—stories of judgment, war, and wrath—have left people confused about God's nature.

But when we view them through Jesus, the perfect image of the Father (Colossians 1:15), everything changes.

God's justice is not about retribution but about restoration.

His wrath is not about destruction but about liberation.

153

And His discipline is not about rejection but about inviting us home.

In this chapter, we'll let Jesus reshape our understanding of God. Through Him, even the Bible's hardest passages come into focus—not as contradictions, but as glimpses of His greater plan.

Jesus Reveals the Father's Heart

For generations, the Jewish people looked to the Law and the Prophets to understand God.

Then Jesus came—and turned their expectations upside down.

They expected retribution—Jesus offered *forgiveness*.

They wanted judgment on sinners—Jesus *ate* with sinners.

They believed God's favor had to be earned—Jesus revealed it as *a gift*.

The Jewish leaders believed the Torah had fully revealed God's justice.

But Jesus showed that they had only seen in part—their understanding was incomplete.

Paul later described how Jesus lifts the veil, revealing the true heart of God:

> *To this day, when Moses is read, a veil lies on their heart.*
> *But whenever one turns to the Lord, the veil is taken away.*
> — *2 Corinthians 3:15–16*

And now, through Him, we are invited to see everything—including the Old Testament—*through new eyes.*

Scripture as a Mirror

One thing we often overlook is that the Bible doesn't just reveal God—it also reveals the human heart.

James describes this beautifully:

> *If anyone is a hearer of the Word and not a doer, he is like someone looking at his natural face in a mirror.*
> *— James 1:23*

Paul goes even further:

> *For the Word of God is living, and active... and is able to discern the thoughts and intentions of the heart.*
> *— Hebrews 4:12*

Here's a hard truth—one few want to accept:

We don't always see Scripture as it is—we often project ourselves onto it.

A tender-hearted person, when wronged, gravitates toward forgiveness passages.

A hardened person, when wronged, finds comfort in verses about vengeance.

Why? Both went through the same experience, yet each saw what *their heart* was inclined toward.

Because Scripture acts as a mirror.

If we fail to put God's Word into practice, we don't truly see God—we only see our own reflection in the pages of Scripture.

We justify our attitudes and project them onto God.

So when we read stories of judgment, war, and destruction, we must pause and ask:

- How does Christ reveal this more clearly?
- Does my interpretation of this passage align with Jesus?

Through Christ's lens, even Scripture's hardest stories reveal a God whose justice seeks restoration, not destruction.

We can now approach Scripture's most difficult passages—not with fear or confusion, but with confidence that Jesus holds the key to understanding them.

So now we begin the longest chapter of the book.

Grab a cup of coffee. Get comfortable.

And let's rediscover the God of the Bible—together.

Eden: Consequences, Not Curses

For many, the story of Adam and Eve is seen as the moment when God's wrath was first revealed—the fall of humanity, followed by divine punishment.

But through Christ's lens, we discover something very different.

This isn't a story of an angry God casting out His children.

It's the story of a loving Father stepping into humanity's brokenness, pointing them toward redemption.

Sin Brings Its Own Consequences

When Adam and Eve disobeyed, they didn't receive a punishment—they stepped outside of life itself.

As Paul writes:

> *For the wages of sin is death.*
> — *Romans 6:23*

This wasn't a legal penalty; it was the natural result of rejecting God, the source of life (John 5:26).

At first glance, it may seem like God is pronouncing a curse.

And from Adam's perspective, it may have felt that way.

But notice God's actual words:

> *Cursed is the ground because of you.*
> — *Genesis 3:17, ESV*

The world was now fractured.

Sin had introduced pain, toil, and death—not as God's punishment, but as the real consequences of separation from Him.

The Poison of Sin

Imagine a bottle of poisonous chemicals under the kitchen sink. On the label, it says: *Fatal if swallowed.*

As a loving parent, you warn your child:

Never drink this—it will kill you.

You even install child locks to protect them.

But one day, you walk into the kitchen and find them drinking it.

Immediately, you rush to rescue them.

You strap them into the car and race to the hospital.

On the way, you explain what's happening:

You're going to feel sick.
Your stomach will hurt.
You might vomit.

Not because you're punishing them, but because the poison is inside them.

This is the story of Eden.

Adam and Eve drank the poison of sin.

And just like that loving parent, God rushed in—not to destroy them, but to save them. He explained what life would now be like in a world touched by sin.

He didn't curse them—He described the consequences of their actions.

They had cursed themselves.

To Adam and Eve, it may have seemed like punishment.

But in reality, God moved swiftly to save them.

He didn't cast them out in anger—He led them forward in love.

The Garden wasn't the moment God's *anger* was revealed —it was the moment His *rescue mission* began.

Noah's Flood: Judgment or Preservation?

Was Noah's flood a story of God's anger and vengeance?

Or was it a story of preservation—a divine act to protect humanity's future?

Before the flood, humanity had spiraled into corruption, oppression, and violence:

God saw that the wickedness of humankind was great on the earth, and that every inclination of the thoughts of his heart was only evil continually.

— Genesis 6:5

Humanity was self-destructing.

Without divine intervention, it would have destroyed itself.

This wasn't just about Noah and his family—it was about God's promise to redeem all of humanity.

From the beginning, God had made a prophetic promise:

I will put enmity between you and the woman, and between your offspring and her Offspring. He will bruise your head, and you will bruise His heel.

— Genesis 3:15

This was the first prophecy of the coming Messiah—the One who would break the power of sin and destroy the works of the devil.

But for that promise to be fulfilled, there had to be a righteous lineage through which the Savior could come.

That's why Scripture makes this stunning declaration:

Noah was a righteous man, blameless among the people of his time. Noah walked with God.

— Genesis 6:9

Noah wasn't just another believer—he and his family were *the last righteous lineage on earth.*

If one more generation had passed, there would have been no one left who walked with God.

No righteous lineage.
No Messiah.
No redemption.

Luke confirms this by including Noah in Christ's genealogy:

> *Jesus... being the son... of Noah... of Adam, of God.*
> *— Luke 3:23–37*

God wasn't just judging sin—**He was protecting the future of salvation itself.**

God's Unbreakable Promise

At this moment in history, God faced an impossible choice:

- **If He did nothing**—humanity would continue its downward spiral. The last righteous family would be lost. The Messiah's lineage would be erased. The promise of salvation would be broken.

- **If He intervened**—He could preserve righteousness, secure the path for the Savior, and extend redemption to all—including those who perished in the flood.

God's promise of redemption was at stake.

If the Savior could not come, *no one—past, present, or future—could be saved.*

God was not acting in vengeance—He was preserving the path of salvation for all generations to come.

Mercy Beyond Judgment

Perhaps the most astonishing revelation about the flood comes from Peter's writings:

> *He* [Jesus] *also went and made a proclamation to the spirits in prison, **who before were disobedient**, when God waited patiently in the days of Noah, while the box-shaped vessel was being built.*
>
> — *1 Peter 3:19–20*

Peter then clarifies the purpose of Christ's proclamation:

> *The Good News was preached to those who are now dead, that they might be judged according to man in the flesh, **but might live according to God in the Spirit**.*
>
> — *1 Peter 4:6*

Did you catch that?

Even those who were disobedient and perished in the flood were not beyond the reach of God's redemption.

God's judgment in the flesh (the flood) became the very doorway for His mercy in the Spirit through Christ—a mercy beyond all human understanding at the time.

Sodom: The Cry of the Oppressed

Sodom and Gomorrah is not just a story of moral failure—it is a story of God confronting systemic oppression.

When two angelic visitors arrived in Sodom, the depravity of the city was fully exposed:

> *The men of the city, the men of Sodom, surrounded the house, both young and old, **all the people from every quarter**. They called to Lot, and said to him, "Where are the men who came in to you this night? Bring them out to us, that we may have sex with them."*
>
> *— Genesis 19:4–5*

Sodom wasn't just sinful—it was a society fueled by exploitation.

A place where the powerful preyed on the vulnerable.
Where violence ruled.
Where oppression wasn't just tolerated—it was expected.
And God heard the cries of the victims:

> *The cry of Sodom and Gomorrah is great, and because their sin is so grievous.*
>
> *— Genesis 18:20*

Who was crying out?
How many had Sodom raped, enslaved, and brutalized?
How many lives had been crushed?

A Righteous Remnant

Just like in the days of Noah, only one righteous family remained.

Abraham interceded with bold compassion:

162

> *Will you sweep away the righteous with the wicked?*
> — *Genesis 18:23*

And what was God's reply?

He would spare the entire city if just ten righteous people could be found.

If even a flicker of hope remained, God would have withheld judgment.

Ezekiel captures God's true heart:

> *"As I live," says the Lord GOD, "I have no pleasure in the death of the wicked; but that the wicked turn from his way and live: turn, turn from your evil ways."*
> — *Ezekiel 33:11*

This wasn't random destruction.

It was divine intervention—a rescue mission to stop unchecked evil and answer the desperate cries of the oppressed.

This is not the story of an angry God wiping out sinners.

It's the story of a loving God who refuses to look away—and steps in to end relentless injustice.

Jesus' Surprising Words About Sodom

Centuries later, Jesus said something astonishing:

> *If the mighty works had been done in Sodom which were done in you, it would have remained until this day.*
> — *Matthew 11:23*

Wait—**what?**

Jesus declared that Sodom would have *repented* if they had seen His miracles.

And He went further:

> *Truly, I say to you, it will be more bearable on the day of judgment for the land of Sodom and Gomorrah than for that town.*
>
> — *Matthew 10:15, ESV*

Did you catch that?

Sodom's destruction was not their final judgment.

Their story was not over.

Just like those in Noah's flood, they too would one day hear the Good News:

> *The Good News was preached to those who are now dead, that they might be judged according to man in the flesh,* **but might live according to God in the Spirit**.
>
> — *1 Peter 4:6*

Yes, God had to end their evil—to stop their relentless oppression of the innocent.

But His justice was never about wiping them out.

It was about stopping the unstoppable.

Even after judgment, His mercy was still at work, reaching beyond death itself.

And if Jesus Himself said Sodom would have repented at His preaching...**what does that reveal about their ultimate destiny?**

Sodom's story shows that God's justice flows from His love:

A love that rescues the innocent.
A love that confronts evil.
A love that extends mercy—even to the disobedient who were judged in the flesh.

This is not unchecked wrath.
It is a testimony to God's relentless pursuit of redemption.

Hyperbole in the Old Testament

One of the greatest challenges in reading the Old Testament is reconciling God's commands to destroy entire nations —men, women, children, infants, and even animals.

How can this align with the God revealed in Christ?

For many, these passages create a distorted image of God— one that appears violent, merciless, and contradictory to Jesus' teachings on love, mercy, and forgiveness.

But what if we've been reading these passages through a modern lens instead of an ancient one?

In the Ancient Near East, *hyperbolic language*—deliberate exaggeration for emphasis—was common, especially in prophecy and accounts of military conquest.

Israel was no exception.

Consider just a few examples where Scripture declares total destruction, yet later reveals survivors:

- Joshua wrote that Israel "left no survivors" (Joshua 10:40), yet we later find many of these same groups still living among the Israelites (Judges 1:21, 27–28).

- Isaiah prophesied of Edom:

Its smoke will go up forever. From generation to generation, it will lie waste. No one will pass through it forever and ever.

— Isaiah 34:10

Yet history confirms that Edom was repopulated and had thriving cities—this was hyperbolic language, not literal.

This was the common ancient language for judgment—meant to communicate *total defeat*, not absolute extermination.

Even Jesus used hyperbole to emphasize spiritual truths:

"If your hand causes you to stumble, cut it off."
— Mark 9:43

Was Jesus advocating self-mutilation? Of course not.
He was using exaggeration to stress the seriousness of sin.
We do the same today:

- It looks like a *bomb* went off in here!
- This is going to take *forever* to clean up!
- They *crushed* them in that game!

This brings us to one of the most difficult and often misunderstood commands in all of Scripture:

God's command to Saul.

Saul and Amalek: What Did God Really Command?

Go and strike Amalek... do not spare them, but kill both man and woman, child and infant, ox and sheep.
— 1 Samuel 15:3

At first glance, this appears to be a command for merciless slaughter.

But when we look closer, we find the familiar marks of hyperbolic language—a call for *decisive victory*, not literal genocide.

Saul spared King Agag (1 Samuel 15:9), and was rebuked—not for failing to kill civilians, but for preserving the leadership of a brutal empire.

Agag was not just any king.

He ruled a violent regime that thrived by raiding the innocent, plundering the helpless, and enslaving the defenseless (Deuteronomy 25:17–18; 1 Samuel 15:33).

By sparing Agag, Saul wasn't showing mercy—he was preserving a system of oppression, ensuring that Amalek's atrocities against women, children, and the elderly would continue.

David: Proof Total Destruction Was Not Literal

If God's command in 1 Samuel 15:3—to completely destroy the Amalekites—was meant *literally*, then David, as Saul's successor, would have been required to carry it out.

After all, God Himself declared: David is *a man after My heart, who will do all My will* (Acts 13:22).

So let's examine David's record:

- **David took livestock as plunder** (1 Samuel 30:18–20)—even though earlier commands said "nothing that breathes" should remain.

- **David spared a third of a defeated population** (2 Samuel 8:2)—demonstrating that God's priority was victory, not extermination.

- **David continued battling the Amalekites** (1 Samuel 30:1,17)—clear evidence they were never fully destroyed.

If Saul had been commanded to wipe out every last Amalekite, then David—who fulfilled all of God's will—would have completed that task.

But he didn't.

These so-called "total destruction" commands were never about genocide.

They were the hyperbolic war language of the ancient world—describing *complete defeat*, not indiscriminate slaughter.

Their goal was to end systemic oppression, not to justify violence against entire populations.

The Lens of Christ: God's Justice

Light passing through a prism reveals a spectrum of colors —colors that were always there, yet hidden until refracted.

Jesus is that prism.

For centuries, people saw glimpses of God, but their vision was blurred.

They saw shadows.

Reflections.

Fragments of the truth.

Many read the Old Testament and see a God of wrath, while the New Testament reveals a God of love.

But Jesus removes the distortion:

No one has seen God at any time. The only Son, who is at the Father's side, has made Him known.
— *John 1:18*

Jesus is not different from the God of the Old Testament—He is the full revelation of who God has always been.

He does not contradict the Old Testament—*He clarifies it.*

Christ Transforms How We See Everything

This lens doesn't just change how we read Scripture—it changes how we see the world.

It gives us:

- **Hope in suffering** – Knowing that even in hardship, God is working to redeem.
- **Assurance in our doubts** – Knowing that God's justice is always guided by His love.
- **Trust in God's purposes** – Even when we don't fully understand them.

The cross reminds us:

Every act of judgment is ultimately aimed at restoration.

Every story of brokenness is part of God's greater plan to redeem all things.

No one's story is over until they stand before Jesus at the final judgment (Revelation 20:11-15).

Whenever one turns to the Lord, the veil is taken away.
— *2 Corinthians 3:16*

169

Will You Look Through His Lens?

Jesus invites us to see God as He truly is.
The veil is lifted.
The mystery is revealed.

God is good.
God is merciful.
God is love.

This is the God who calls us:

Not just to understanding, but to awe.
Not just to belief, but to adoration.
A story like this was never meant to be explained from a distance.
It was meant to be entered, embraced, and echoed with every breath and every beat of our hearts.
And now—we respond.

With worship.

Reflection and Study Guide

Chapter 10: Christ—The True Lens to See God

He is the radiance of His glory, the very image of His substance, and upholding all things by the Word of His power. — Hebrews 1:3

Questions for Reflection

- **Jesus as the True Revelation:** How does seeing Jesus as the full revelation of God reshape how you interpret difficult Old Testament passages?

- **The Purpose of Judgment:** In what ways do stories like Noah's flood or Sodom and Gomorrah reveal that God's justice is aimed at redemption rather than destruction?

- **Hyperbole and Context:** How does recognizing ancient hyperbole reshape how we view Old Testament passages in light of Christ's character?

Key Takeaways

- **Jesus Reveals God Fully:** Christ is the clearest image of God's heart, lifting the veil on how we understand divine justice, mercy, and love (John 1:18; Colossians 1:15).

- **Judgment Aimed at Redemption:** Stories like the flood, Sodom and Gomorrah, and the conquest narratives show that God's justice is never about destruction for its own sake but about preserving His redemptive plan.

- **Reading Scripture in Context:** Ancient hyperbole and cultural context help us understand that Old Testament war language was not about genocide but about total victory over oppression.

Practical Application

- **Read with Christ's Lens:** Choose a difficult Old Testament passage this week (e.g., the flood, Sodom and Gomorrah, or the conquest of Canaan). Ask: How does Jesus reveal God's justice and mercy in this story?

- **Embody Justice and Mercy:** In your daily life, look for ways to reflect God's justice and mercy. Is there someone who needs both accountability and grace from you? How can you model Christ's love?

- **Worship the God Revealed in Christ:** Spend time in worship, thanking God that His justice is ultimately redemptive. Reflect on how this truth brings peace and trust in His character.

Conclusion: Worshiping the God Who Is Love

Worship: The Heartbeat of Our Existence

Worship is our deepest calling. It is not just something we do—it is who we are created to be.

From the moment of creation, we were designed to live in awe, wonder, and communion with God.

At the deepest level, every human heart longs for something greater, something eternal.

This longing is not random.

It is the pull of our Creator drawing us back to Himself.

Worship is not about performing religious duties or offering God something He lacks.

It is about responding to the One who first loved us, surrendering to the beauty of who He is, and embracing His presence as the very source of life.

Worship is not just singing—it is seeing.

It is the soul awakened to the reality of God's love, power, and holiness.

It is standing in awe of the Father.

It is beholding the glory of the Son.

It is being transformed by the Spirit.

And when we worship in spirit and in truth, we step into the very life of the Trinity itself.

The God We Were Created to Worship

This book has been a journey—not just through theology, but through the heart of God.

We have explored the fullness of the Father, Son, and Spirit —perfect in unity, inseparable in love, working together in power.

We have seen that atonement is not about satisfying wrath but restoring relationship.

That salvation is not a legal exchange but a cosmic rescue.

That the Trinity is not a puzzle to be solved but the very life we are called to enter.

Now, the journey reaches its climax—not in explanation, *but in response.*

Worship is not the end of theology.

It is its fulfillment.

The call is not just to know the Trinity but to live within the Trinity—to be drawn into the eternal love of God.

And when we truly see Him, we cannot help but worship.

Worshiping the Triune God

Honoring the Father: The Source of All Worship

The Father is the fountainhead of all life, the One from whom all things flow.

When Jesus taught us to pray, *Our Father in Heaven, holy be Your name* (Matthew 6:9), He was reorienting our hearts toward the ultimate reality—God as the source of all things.

To worship the Father is to stand in awe of His holiness, majesty, and sovereignty.

Yet, incredibly, this same Father invites us to come near—not as slaves, but as beloved children.

Glorifying the Son: The Revelation of the Father

Jesus Christ is the visible image of the invisible God.
He did not come to change the Father's heart toward us—He came to reveal it.

> *No one comes to the Father except through Me.*
> *— John 14:6*

Through Christ, worship moves beyond duty to *intimacy*.
We do not approach God from a distance—we are brought near, made righteous by the Son, standing in the embrace of divine love.
To worship Jesus is to worship the Father.
To behold the Son is to see the very heart of God.

Worshiping in the Spirit: God's Presence in Us

> *God is spirit, and those who worship Him must worship in spirit and truth.*
> *— John 4:24*

The Spirit does not merely lead us to worship—He is the very presence of God within us, making worship possible.
Without the Spirit, worship is a cold ritual.
With the Spirit, worship becomes an *encounter*.
He stirs our hearts.
He opens our eyes.

He transforms our very being until worship is no longer just something we do—it is the atmosphere in which we live.

To worship in the Spirit is to be caught up in the life of God Himself.

Gratitude: The Heart of True Worship

At its core, worship is not obligation—it is gratitude.

It is the heart overwhelmed by love.

It is the soul awakened to grace.

It is the voice that cannot stay silent in the presence of glory.

> *What will I give to the LORD for all His benefits toward me? I will take the cup of salvation, and call on the name of the LORD.*
>
> *— Psalm 116:12–13*

We do not worship to get something from God.

We worship because He has *already* given us everything.

Every moment of joy, every answered prayer, every breath we take—these are invitations to praise.

Gratitude transforms life itself into an act of worship.

Every prayer becomes a song.

Every struggle becomes an offering.

Every heartbeat becomes a hallelujah.

A Glimpse into Eternity

One day, the veil will be lifted.

The struggles will end.
The distractions will fade.
And we will see the One our souls have longed for.

> *Holy, holy, holy is the Lord God Almighty, who was and who is and who is to come.*
>
> — *Revelation 4:8*

In that moment, every shadow will vanish.
Every tear will be wiped away.
Every longing will be fulfilled.
We will see Him face to face.
We will know Him as we are known.
We will be fully alive in the life of the Trinity, forever.

The Call to Worship Now

But we don't have to wait for eternity to begin worshiping.
The call to worship is now.
The invitation stands before you now.
The Father is seeking worshipers—not spectators, not distant admirers, but those who will enter into His presence, abide in His love, and declare His glory.
Let your worship reflect the truth revealed in this book:

- That God has made Himself fully known in Christ.

- That salvation is not escape, but restoration.

- That the Trinity is not a theory but the very life we are called to enter.

This is the God who loves you.
This is the God who is worthy of your worship.

To Him who sits on the throne, and to the Lamb be the blessing, the honor, the glory, and the dominion, forever and ever.

— Revelation 5:13

So lift your heart.
Lift your voice.
Lift your life.

For He is worthy.

Appendix A: Councils, Heresies, and This Book

What the Early Councils Sought to Protect

Throughout Church history, doctrinal controversies arose that clarified truth—but also stirred confusion.

In response, the early ecumenical councils were not convened to invent doctrine, but to guard the Gospel from distortion.

Their creeds, forged in the fires of dispute, were heroic in affirming foundational truths:

- **The oneness of God.**
- **The full divinity of Christ.**
- **The Trinitarian nature of salvation.**

Yet over time, many of the *scriptural concerns* behind the heresies they addressed remained unresolved—not because the councils were indifferent, but because their tools were philosophical rather than pastoral or exegetical.

This appendix affirms the value of the councils by showing:

- What they sought to protect—and why it mattered.
- Why confusion kept resurfacing.
- How this book's model affirms their doctrinal outcomes while avoiding Greek metaphysics and addressing the biblical concerns others overlooked.

The Key Councils and What They Fought For

Council	Date	Main Purpose	Defending
Nicaea I	325 AD	Counter Arianism	Jesus is fully God, "of one substance" (*homoousios*) with the Father.
Constantinople I	381 AD	Clarify the Divinity of the Spirit	The Holy Spirit is fully divine and personal—not a created force.
Ephesus	431 AD	Counter Nestorianism	Jesus is one person—fully divine and fully human, not two persons joined together.
Chalcedon	451 AD	Define the Hypostatic Union	Christ is one person in two natures—divine and human—without confusion or division.
Constantinople II	553 AD	Reaffirm Nicene-Chalcedonian Theology	Christ's two natures remain united in one person; condemned subtle Nestorian errors.
Constantinople III	681 AD	Address Christ's Will(s)	Christ has two wills—human and divine—working in full harmony, not opposition.

This Model: Upholding Truth While Restoring Clarity

The councils sought to protect the right things: the mystery of Christ and the unity of the Triune God.

Their motivation was rooted in preserving the heart of the Christian faith.

But the model presented in this book accomplishes what their conclusions—limited by Greek philosophy—could not:

- **It answers the *scriptural* concerns** raised by groups like the Arians and Nestorians—not by dismissing them as heretics, but by engaging their arguments with biblical clarity.

- **It affirms *every* core doctrine** upheld by the councils: Christ's divinity, unity with the Father, full humanity, and the relational harmony of the Trinity.

- **It avoids the *confusion* of Greek philosophy**, offering instead the relational narrative that unfolds naturally throughout Scripture.

This model doesn't redefine what the councils fought for—*it fulfills their intention.*

It offers a vision of the Trinity that is biblically faithful, spiritually compelling, and relationally coherent.

Four Key Heresies—and What They Missed

Throughout Church history, sincere attempts to understand the mystery of God often drifted into error—not from rebellion, but from genuine questions left unanswered by a Scripture-focused theology.

Still, some conclusions led to distortions the Church was compelled to confront.

These include:

Heresy	Main Claim	The Core Oversight
Arianism Nicaea I (325)	Jesus was a created being and therefore not fully divine.	Raised valid scriptural concerns, but the Church's response relied on Greek philosophical categories.
Modalism All Councils	One God appearing in three modes—at different times, but not simultaneously.	Emphasized Old Testament oneness but ignored the relational distinctions revealed in the Incarnation.
Tritheism All Councils	Three separate divine beings cooperating in unity —a family of gods.	Prioritized New Testament distinctions but fractured God's essential oneness.
Nestorianism Ephesus (431)	Jesus existed as two distinct persons— one divine (the *Logos*), one human.	Split Christ's personhood; the council rightly affirmed His unity but lacked scriptural clarity.

Why This Model Holds Fast Where Others Fractured

This model affirms every truth the early councils sought to protect:

- **One God.**
- **Three Persons.**
- **Christ fully divine and fully human.**
- **The Spirit truly God.**

But it does so without philosophical confusion—offering precise, scriptural answers to the core concerns behind each historical heresy.

Below are four major heresies—each followed by how this

model answers the heart of their concern through the lens of Scripture alone.

- **Arianism** – *Denied Christ's full divinity, treating Him as a created being.*

The eternal Word is uncreated—fully God from the beginning. His personal distinction *as Son* began in time through the Incarnation, but the Word is eternally divine.

- **Modalism** – *Flattened God's relational life into roles, denying personal distinction.*

This model reveals real relational distinction: the Father remains the source, the Word becomes the Son through the Incarnation, and the Spirit becomes personally distinct at Christ's Glorification—not mere roles, but persons in loving unity, revealed in time.

- **Tritheism** – *Divided God into three separate beings, undermining oneness.*

This model preserves divine unity: one will, one essence, one life—flowing from the Father, through the Son, by the Spirit. The Trinity is relationally revealed, never divided.

- **Nestorianism** – *Split Christ into two persons, fracturing His unity.*

The Word did not join Himself to an existing human being; He became a full human life—spirit, soul, and body. Not two selves, but one unified Person, fully God and fully man.

183

Other Lingering Errors Addressed

- **Subordinationism** – *Treated the Son or Spirit as eternally inferior in nature (not just role).*

This model shows submission in mission, not essence—equal in divinity, distinct in role.

- **Patripassianism** – *Confused Father and Son, portraying the Father as suffering on the cross.*

The Father did not suffer death on the cross. The Son, fully human and the radiance of the Father, suffered and died—real distinction without division.

- **Binitarianism** – *Reducing the Spirit to a force or merely Christ's presence, instead of recognizing Him as a distinct divine person.*

The Spirit is not a force. He is the shared life of the Father and glorified Son—now personally present within us.

- **Adoptionism** – *Claimed Jesus became the Son at Baptism or Resurrection.*

Jesus was not *made* the Son—He *became* the Son when the eternal Word took on human life through the Incarnation.

- **Docetism** – *Denied Christ's true humanity by claiming He only appeared human.*

Jesus was not an illusion—He was fully human: body, soul, and will, capable of suffering, growth, and obedience.

- **Apollinarianism** – *Claimed that Christ had a divine mind but no human soul.*

The Word did not override a human soul. He assumed a full human psyche: intellect, emotion, and volition.

- **Monophysitism** – *Collapsing Christ's humanity into His divinity, denying two full natures.*

Christ's humanity was not erased—His two natures remain whole and distinct in one unified person.

- **Monothelitism** – *Denied Christ had a human will.*

Jesus possessed both a divine will [Spirit] and a human will [flesh]. His obedience was not automatic—it was fully and freely submitted.

- **Functional Tritheism** – *Treated each Person of the Trinity as having a separate divine will, dividing God into three centers of consciousness.*

God does not operate as a divine committee. This model affirms one divine will—expressed through Father, Son, and Spirit in perfect unity.

More Than Theological Precision—Pastoral Restoration

This isn't about labeling errors.

It's about answering the *real questions* those errors raised —not with borrowed systems, but through the framework Scripture itself provides.

The early councils gave us the guardrails.

This model builds a road within them—anchored in Scripture, alive in the Spirit, and centered on Christ.

What this book has done is simple but significant:

> **It removes the Trinity from Greek philosophical categories and re-centers it within the unfolding story of Scripture—just as the Early Church did in its first three centuries.**

Tertullian, writing in the late second century, affirmed that relational roles like "Father" and "Son" began in time. (*See Appendix B*).

This doesn't reduce mystery—it removes contradiction and restores Early Church clarity.

> **One God.**
> **Revealed as Father, Son, and Spirit.**

Appendix B: The True Fathers of the Trinity

Theophilus and Tertullian

If the councils gave us the framework, and the heresies revealed the cracks, then the early witnesses—*Theophilus and Tertullian*—help us rediscover the foundation.

Writing more than a century before the Council of Nicaea, both men articulated a Trinitarian faith that predated all official creeds and carried no trace of later Greek metaphysical categories—such as timeless essence, eternal generation, or co-equal persons.

In fact, both explicitly rejected Plato's assumptions as unscriptural, insisting that God's nature must be defined by Scripture, not philosophy.

> *Heresies are themselves instigated by philosophy... The apostle would restrain us, he expressly names philosophy as that which he would have us be on our guard against. Writing to the Colossians, he says, "See that no one beguile you through philosophy..." What concord is there between the Academy* [the school of Plato] *and the Church? What between heretics and Christians... Away with all attempts to produce a mottled Christianity of Stoic, Platonic, and dialectic composition!*
>
> — Tertullian, *Prescription Against Heretics*, Chapter 7

> *What did Plato's system of culture profit him? Or what benefit did the rest of the philosophers derive from their*

doctrines... But... for the purpose of exhibiting their useless and godless opinions... neither themselves knew the truth, nor guided others to the truth.

— Theophilus of Antioch, *To Autolycus*, Book 3, Chapter 2-3

These two were the first Christians to coin the term Trinity —Theophilus in Greek (*Trias*) around 180 AD, and Tertullian in Latin (*Trinitas*) around 213 AD.

Theophilus introduced the term while reflecting on the creation account in Genesis:

The luminaries [sun, moon, and stars], *are types of the Trinity, of God* [like the sun in unapproachable glory], *and His Word* [like the moon, reflecting the Father's light in a form we can behold], *and His wisdom* [like the stars, shining everywhere at once].

— Theophilus of Antioch, *To Autolycus*, Book 2, Chapter 15

Tertullian likewise coined Trinitas—not as a puzzle of three co-eternal persons, but as the unfolding revelation of one God who speaks, sends, and indwells.

In *Against Praxeas*, he developed the earliest Latin framework for the Trinity and defended it with biblical clarity against both modalism and tritheism.

Though widely revered in Church history, Tertullian's understanding of the Trinity was not the static, philosophical formula inherited by later tradition.

He described God's self-revelation as an *oikonomia*—a divine order or plan in which the Father, Son, and Spirit emerge relationally in redemptive history.

Together, Theophilus and Tertullian are the true fathers of

the Trinity—not merely because they coined the term, but because they defended it on biblical grounds, free from the Greek metaphysics that would later obscure their intent.

They offer a vision of God that is dynamic, relational, and redemptive—not defined by abstract essence or timeless speculation, but by the living story of God's unfolding self-revelation.

Tertullian's Trinitarian Vision

God Becomes Father and Judge in Time

> *God is in like manner a Father, and He is also a Judge; but He has not always been Father and Judge, merely on the ground of His having always been God. For He could not have been the Father previous to the Son, nor a Judge previous to sin.*
>
> — Tertullian, *Against Hermogenes*, Chapter 3

Tertullian rejects the idea that God's roles are timeless abstractions. Instead, He becomes Father through the generation of the Son, and Judge when sin enters the world.

The Logos Was in God Before Proceeding from God

> *Before all things God was alone... Yet even not then was He alone; for He had with Him that which He possessed in Himself, that is to say, His own Reason [Logos].*
>
> — Tertullian, *Against Praxeas*, Chapter 5

Tertullian affirms that the Word [Logos] existed eternally

within God as His own Reason—divine but not personally distinct until He proceeded forth for creation and redemption.

The Son Was Generated When God Willed

> *He became also the Son of God, and was begotten when He proceeded forth from Him* [the Father].
>
> — Tertullian, *Against Praxeas*, Chapter 7

Tertullian presents no concept of eternal generation. The Son becomes personally distinct by God's will, not by timeless necessity. Sonship begins with the act of procession—not as an eternal condition.

The Distinction Is in Role, Not in Substance

> *While the mystery of the dispensation is still guarded, which distributes the Unity into a Trinity, placing in their order the three Persons— the Father, the Son, and the Holy Ghost: three, however, not in condition, but in degree; not in substance, but in form; not in power, but in aspect; yet of one substance, and of one condition, and of one power, inasmuch as He is one God, from whom these degrees and forms and aspects are reckoned, under the name of the Father, and of the Son, and of the Holy Ghost.*
>
> — Tertullian, *Against Praxeas*, Chapter 2

Tertullian affirms unity of being but diversity in function and appearance—using *personae* in the Roman sense of role or legal standing, not as later theology defined "person" as an eternal self. His framework is relational and historical, not metaphysical.

The Spirit Proceeds Through the Son

Who derive the Son from no other source but from the substance of the Father... I believe the Spirit to proceed from no other source than from the Father through the Son.

— Tertullian, *Against Praxeas*, Chapter 4

Tertullian envisions a divine flow—Father —> Son —> Spirit—that reflects the biblical pattern and aligns with the theology presented in this book.

The Trinity Flows from God's Economy (Oikonomia)

We... believe that there is one only God, but under the following dispensation, or οἰκονομία, as it is called, that this one only God has also a Son, His Word, who proceeded from Himself, by whom all things were made, and without whom nothing was made.

— Tertullian, *Against Praxeas*, Chapter 2

Tertullian roots the Trinity not in abstract substance meta-physics, but in God's oikonomia—His ordered plan of self-revelation through the Son and Spirit.

This is not eternal division but historical distinction in the one unfolding mission of God.

Summary: Two Witnesses, One Vision

While we have fewer surviving writings from Theophilus, his theology displays remarkable harmony with Tertullian's.

Theophilus was the first theologian to:

- Coin the word Trias (Greek for Trinity).

- Illustrate the Trinity through creation—presenting the sun, moon, and stars as types of God, His Word, and His Wisdom.

- Affirm that God made all things by His Word and Wisdom—not by abstract essence (*To Autolycus* II.10).

- Teach that God is revealed progressively: first in creation, then through His Word, and ultimately through Christ.

- Reject the authority of poets and philosophers, insisting that Scripture is the true source of knowledge.

- Present the Trinity as a historical revelation of God's nature and mission.

Tertullian was the first theologian to:

- Coin the word Trinitas (Latin for Trinity).

- Define the Father, Son, and Spirit not as three co-eternal persons, but as one divine substance revealed in three ordered distinctions through the divine economy (oikonomia).

- Reject both modalism (one person in three modes) and tritheism (three gods).

- Root the Trinity in God's redemptive plan, not in abstract philosophy.

Together, Theophilus and Tertullian are early witnesses to a Trinity that is alive, relational, and revealed—not through Greek speculation, but through Scripture and salvation history.

Their voices still speak—not as relics of a primitive faith, but as reformers calling us back to the source.

Final Reflection: What Was Lost

The Council of Nicaea, as shown in *Appendix A*, rightly defended the divinity of Christ and the oneness of God.

For that, it deserves honor.

This appendix, however, exists to show what was lost in the process.

What Theophilus and Tertullian explicitly rejected—Greek philosophical categories—became the very building blocks of orthodoxy.

As Augustine would later write:

> *If those who are called philosophers, and especially the Platonists, have said anything that is true and in harmony with our faith, we are not only not to shrink from it, but to* **claim it for our own use**.
>
> — Augustine, *On Christian Doctrine*, Book 2, Chapter 40

With that, the shift was complete.

The Church did not merely drift from its early witnesses—it completely reversed their warnings. And as Theophilus cautioned, when we exchange the voice of revelation for the reasoning of philosophy, *we inherit its contradictions*.

In that reversal, the Church didn't just forget its roots—it buried them.

Theophilus and Tertullian were the first to name the Trinity. But they did more than coin a term—they offered a vision of God grounded in Scripture, not speculation.

Now, two thousand years later, their voices rise again—calling the Church to return to the God who reveals Himself not through metaphysics, but through story.

This book seeks to recover what was lost.

It honors the essential truths defended by the councils—but it reclaims them by returning to the biblical clarity and pastoral intent of these two men:

The true fathers of the Trinity.

Appendix C: The Apostles' Creed

The Early Church Creed Unshaped by Greek Philosophy

The *Apostles' Creed* is one of the earliest and clearest expressions of the Christian faith.

This Creed was not born from controversy or defense, but from baptismal confession and unity. It reflects the heartbeat of the Gospel as it was believed and proclaimed by the apostles themselves—*simple, clear, and Trinitarian.*

Unlike the later creeds, shaped in the fires of theological debate and philosophical frameworks, this Creed flows from the lived experience of the Early Church.

It was not crafted to argue, but to anchor.

It gave early believers a shared confession of faith—rooted in Scripture, empowered by the Spirit, and shaped by story.

It declares the glory of the Father, reveals the work of the Son, and celebrates the indwelling power of the Spirit.

This early Creed contains the seeds of the entire Gospel.

Read in light of God's unfolding revelation—culminating in Christ and extended through the Spirit—it becomes more than a statement to affirm; it becomes a story to live.

Rooted in Scripture and the Early Church's lived experience, this Creed is the theological center of gravity for everything this book explores.

What follows is the original Creed in bold, each line followed by a theological reflection and supporting Scriptures.

I believe in God, the Father almighty, creator of Heaven and Earth;

The transcendent Father is the one true God—uncaused, eternal, and self-existent—from whom are all things and for whom we exist. He is the source of life and love, who created all things in wisdom, and upholds the world by His word.

John 17:3, 1 Corinthians 8:6, Hebrews 1:3

I believe in Jesus Christ His only Son our Lord; He was conceived by the power of the Holy Spirit, and born of the Virgin Mary,

The eternal Word was with the Father in the beginning, His radiant self-expression in creation and covenant. In the fullness of time, the Word became flesh—truly God and truly human—the only begotten Son who reveals the Father's heart. He is the image of the invisible God, full of grace and truth.

John 1:1, 14, 18, Luke 1:35, Hebrews 1:1–3, Colossians 1:15

He suffered under Pontius Pilate, was crucified, died, and was buried. He descended to the dead.

In faithfulness to the Father, He submitted to suffering and death, bearing the weight of sin and death's dominion. He fully entered the human condition, even unto Sheol, the place of the dead. Yet He descended not in defeat, but in triumph—proclaiming victory to the spirits in captivity and breaking the grip of the grave.

Isaiah 53:4–6, Romans 5:8, Acts 2:31, Ephesians 4:9–10, 1 Peter 3:18–19

On the third day He rose again. He ascended into Heaven, and is seated at the right hand of the Father. He will come again to judge the living and the dead.

He rose in glorified humanity, having conquered death by death. He ascended in power, and now reigns at the Father's right hand as King, Priest, and Intercessor. From His throne of glorified authority, He pours out His Spirit upon His Body, the Church, and will come again to set all things right—to judge the nations, restore justice, reveal mercy, and make all things new.

Philippians 2:9–11, Acts 2:33, Romans 8:34, Hebrews 9:28, Revelation 21:5

I believe in the Holy Spirit,

The eternal Spirit is the breath of the living God, hovering at creation, speaking through the prophets, and coming upon God's people throughout the ages. Poured out anew through the risen Christ, the Spirit now indwells the Church—forming us as the Body of Christ, the dwelling place of the Triune God.

Genesis 1:2, John 7:39, Romans 8:9–11, Acts 2:33, 1 Corinthians 3:16

The holy universal Church, the communion of saints,

The Church is the new creation community—those called out and united in the Spirit, made holy by grace and formed in Christ to bear His image. We are joined across time and space, called to reflect the Father's glory and participate in the mission of the Son.

Ephesians 4:4–6, 1 Peter 2:9–10, Matthew 28:18–20, Hebrews 12:22–24

The forgiveness of sins,

In Christ's death and Resurrection, sin is overcome, and estrangement is healed. Through Him, we are reconciled to the Father, washed by grace, and empowered by the Spirit to live as new creations. Forgiveness is not mere pardon, but the restoration of communion with God.

Romans 5:9–11, Titus 3:5–7, 1 John 1:9, 2 Corinthians 5:17–21

The resurrection of the body, and the life everlasting. Amen.

As Christ was raised, so shall we. Mortality will put on immortality, and creation itself will be renewed. Even now, the Spirit is restoring all things through the Church, the firstfruits of the new creation. He is subduing every enemy under Christ's feet, until death is no more. Then the Son will hand all things to the Father, that God may be all in all.

1 Corinthians 15:20–28, Romans 8:11, 19–21, Revelation 21:1–5

This Creed anchors the vision of the Trinity this book seeks to recover—a God who reveals Himself not through abstract categories, but through story: in creation, in Christ, and now in us. It reminds us that the Trinity is not a concept to master, but a communion to join—a living story we are invited to enter.

Bibliography

Ancient Christian Sources

- **Justin Martyr** (c. 155 AD). *Second Apology*, Chapter 6. Trans. Marcus Dods and George Reith. Accessed at New Advent: https://www.newadvent.org/fathers/0127.htm

- **Irenaeus of Lyons** (c. 180 AD). *Against Heresies*, Book II, Chapter 32; Book IV, Preface; and Book V, Chapter 18. Trans. Alexander Roberts and William Rambaut. Accessed at New Advent: https://www.newadvent.org/fathers/0103.htm

- **Theophilus of Antioch** (c. 180 AD). *To Autolycus*, Book II, Chapter 15; and Book III, Chapters 2–4. Trans. Marcus Dods. Accessed at New Advent: https://www.newadvent.org/fathers/0204.htm

- **Tertullian** (c. 200 AD). *Against Hermogenes*, Chapter 3. Trans. Peter Holmes. Accessed at New Advent: https://www.newadvent.org/fathers/0313.htm

- **Tertullian** (c. 205 AD). *Prescription Against Heretics*, Chapter 7. Trans. Peter Holmes. Accessed at New Advent: https://www.newadvent.org/fathers/0311.htm

- **Tertullian** (c. 213 AD). *Against Praxeas*, Chapters 2, 4, 5, and 7. Trans. Peter Holmes. Accessed at New Advent: https://www.newadvent.org/fathers/0317.htm

- **Origen** (c. 220 AD). *Against Celsus*, Book I, Chapter 46. Trans. Frederick Crombie. Accessed at New Advent: https://www.newadvent.org/fathers/04161.htm

- **Basil the Great** (c. 375 AD). *On the Holy Spirit*, Chapter 15.36. Trans. Blomfield Jackson. Accessed at New Advent: https://www.newadvent.org/fathers/3203.htm

- **Gregory of Nyssa** (c. 380 AD). *On "Not Three Gods"*. Trans. H.A. Wilson. Accessed at New Advent: https://www.newadvent.org/fathers/2905.htm

- **Augustine of Hippo** (397 AD). *On Christian Doctrine*, Book II, Chapter 40. Trans. James Shaw. Accessed at New Advent: https://www.newadvent.org/fathers/12022.htm

- **Augustine of Hippo** (c. 420 AD). *The City of God*, Book XXII, Chapter 8. Trans. Marcus Dods. Accessed at New Advent: https://www.newadvent.org/fathers/120122.htm